RAMBLINGS

Henderson

EMMA BICKHAM PITCHER

RAMBLINGS

REFLECTIONS ON NATURE

ILLUSTRATED BY
ELIZABETH HENDERSON

BEECH LEAF PRESS
KALAMAZOO, MICHIGAN

Library of Congress Catalog Card Number:
00-136100
ISBN 0-939294-14-2
Printed in the United States of America

For
Floyd A. Swink
1921-2000

Wise Mentor
Warm Friend

Contents

Out and About

Introduction

WHEN I WAS A LITTLE GIRL, we picnicked in the forest preserves west of Wilmette, Illinois, or on our nearby Lake Michigan beach. In the years since then, I've made my home in five states, spent thousands of hours tramping up, down, and around twenty-three others, rambled at length over German woods and fields, and wandered Arctic tundra for seven summers. Always the lure is the same: go outdoors to see what bird, flower, or tree is new, puzzling, or beautiful.

Eventually the urge to celebrate what I've experienced surfaces and another essay is born. Somehow, the need to communicate grows stronger as threats to whatever wildness is left continue unabated. Populations expand, cities sprawl, pristine wildness is compromised. Pollution prevails. Tough and fertile alien plants multiply. What can I write that might prompt someone to be intrigued by the myriad wonders out there and want to work toward saving them? What more can we do to help preserve natural areas?

This book is dedicated to Floyd A. Swink (1921-2000), long-time mentor and friend. His untimely death deprived us all of a leading taxonomist and a consummate punster. For over forty-five years I was privileged to walk in his footsteps in Door County, Wisconsin's cedar woods, in Illinois forest preserves, and in the Indiana Dunes.

These essays have been written since late 1995, and were published in the weekly Kalamazoo Nature Center "Nature's Way" column in the Kalamazoo *Gazette*. The earlier work, *Of Wood and Other Things*, contains a bibliography to which interested readers can refer.

Scientific terms are not used in the text, but are linked to common names in the glossary. Although the hyphen is currently used in many common names, some have been deleted. Both actions should result in easier reading.

During the past few years, several people have asked me: Are you going to publish another book? Friends say that the short essay format makes for good bedtime reading—a chapter a night. We hope that will be true for you, too.

About Birds

Verbs for Birds

WHAT VERBS WOULD YOU use to describe the movement of birds? We all know a duck waddles because his legs are situated so far back on his body. And a mute swan trying to get his twenty-five pounds airborne has to thrash and thrash the water heavily. What other verbs immediately remind you of some particular avian experience you have had?

The word bounce connotes a sprightly reaction—the thing a tennis ball does after being hit by Pete Sampras or Martina Hingis. I think a saucy-demeanored black-capped chickadee bounces—he levitates in defiance of gravity. It's almost as if there were built-in springs in his legs that make possible his fast takeoffs. Bounce has other meanings relating to bad checks, night club guards, office dismissals, illness recoveries, but I like best to think of it describing the effortless verve of a chickadee's departure from a feeder.

Some bird groups explode, really frightening an unaware passerby. Ruffed grouse and Gambel's quail broods, cornered or threatened, will burst out suddenly from under one's feet—birds everywhere, flying in a dramatic distraction display.

Hovering is fascinating avian behavior to watch. You wonder if you're seeing things. If an airplane were to try standing still on air, it wouldn't work; its aeronautical dynamics would be destroyed and it would become an FAA statistic. But some birds—from hummers to rough-legged hawks, including terns, kestrels, and kingfishers—can hover, beating their wings rapidly to keep the same position while checking out a possible meal. Hummingbirds, the most successful of all hovering species, seem to stand still as they suck nectar from a flower, maintaining the position with as many as seventy beats per second, wing beats too fast for human eyes to see anything but a blur. A belted kingfisher poises, wings beating hard; then, when ready to dive, he closes his wings tight to his body and plunges into the water. He may also perch motionless in a conspicuous place, waiting for a meal to appear before he dives.

Eagles may dive from high in the air, making spectacular plunges several feet into the water. Gannets, too, do high dives, fifty feet or more, when in search of quarry.

Thornton Burgess, and other children's authors who anthropomorphised many animals, wrote of Sammy Jay strutting and swaggering. I think swoop is a fitting verb for him. Many birds approach feeders in short reconnaissance stages, making sure the runway is clear, before making the final approach. But not the blue jay. He swoops rapidly, gulps down one to fifteen seeds, and vanishes, scattering smaller birds willy-nilly.

Pounce is another descriptive but useful verb describing particular bird movements. A robin will cruise around a lawn in dignified fashion, head cocked, but when the right moment occurs, that yellow bill goes after the worm with considerable strength and style. He pounces on it. Similarly, a perched barn owl or great gray owl studies the ground intently, and then, with a graceful whoosh, the bird plummets down, and another rodent becomes dinner. Kestrels on telephone wires have similar performances.

What is it to soar? Is it to float through the air, wings rigid, stiffly extended, body hardly moving, taking advantage of wind currents to maintain or increase altitude? A barely discernible rocking or tilting from side to side helps maintain position. To see hawks endlessly circling in larger and larger arcs as they rise on thermals, the heat currents coming up from the land, is always mind-boggling to me.

Anyone fortunate enough to find adult birds feeding their young experiences perfect examples of begging. With mouth agape and wings flapping wildly, the fledgling entreats a harried parent to feed him immediately. One can almost feel saliva running, so violent is the activity.

During May migration, enjoying a small flowering

tree alive with wood warblers—black and white and yellow flashing everywhere—is to experience the act of flitting. We were watching such an enchanting tree once, dashing back and forth, binoculars up and down, shouting excited "oh looks", trying to get one set of wings in focus, when an unknown cartoonist's prototype of an elderly female birdwatcher in tennis shoes said to us; "Forget your binoculars. Stand still and just watch for field marks." Her advice worked. We let the birds do the flitting.

A nighthawk in dramatic courtship display flight booms with his wings as he makes a spectacular plunge from high in the air. The sound is the rapid rush vibrating the feathers.

Birds that spend most of their time in trees generally hop with both feet whether in the tree or on the ground. This is tiring because the entire weight has to be lifted every time. Ground nesters such as meadowlarks are more apt to walk, one leg moving at a time, and the entire weight is never suspended. Brown creepers and white-breasted nuthatches creep up and down and around trunks while woodpeckers hitch their way up.

To see a flight of gulls leisurely beating their way down a wind-driven, sunlit lake is a pleasant sight, evocative of summer days. The effortless flight is the evidence of having a complete set of all the necessary equipment and having it in perfect working condition.

A male ruffed grouse drums with his wings, using the whirring sound to stake out his territory, repelling other males and attracting females. Many birds glide effortlessly into landings, making no body movements, just coasting downhill, wings extended, legs down ready to make contact.

Black skimmers skim and roadrunners run and. . .

November 29, 1997

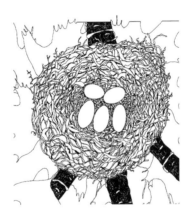

Eastern Screech Owl

EASTERN SCREECH OWLS, like barred and great horned owls, are permanent residents in southwest Michigan. Because they are active at night, they are not often seen by casual observers. In winter, these engaging little birds roost in holes in dead trees and wood duck nest boxes. They sit in entry holes in plain sight for hours at a time, sometimes with eyes open, but often as not, with them closed, apparently napping.

One wonders how they can possibly find enough live prey in hard winters when snow cover can last for weeks. The bird's large and varied diet consists of insects, frogs, small birds, mice, and other little furry mammals. Considering this bird's eight-inch size, just smaller than a robin, it speaks to the strength and design of his body. With his hooked beak, short heavy legs, and sharp curved talons, he can control a frog or bird well enough to catch and eat it.

Pellets, indigestible parts of food, are regurgitated about two hours after eating. United States Fish and Wildlife Service bands, from legs of small birds they have eaten, are occasionally found in castings along with crushed bits of bone and fur fragments.

Like several other owls, these have ear tufts which are not ears at all. Completely hidden behind feathers, their ears are really holes in the side of the head. Tufts may reflect sound, helping to locate prey in low light conditions.

For reasons ornithologists don't really understand, there are two color phases—or morphs—of screech owl plumage, red and gray, with gray-colored feathers more common. These two colors occur throughout the bird's range, without regard to age or sex, and remain the same during its entire life. Broods often have both colors among four or five nestlings.

Staring round eyes, like those of all owls, are unique and fascinating in their special adaptations for night vision. Yellow pupils expand to cover most of the eyeball. Because the eye is immovable in its socket, this owl instead turns his head almost 280 degrees, which he does with such smooth speed one is scarcely aware of any movement.

Nests are always in holes and no lining material is used. Females lay four or five round white eggs and incubate them for twenty-six days. The male feeds her on the nest. After the young hatch, the nest floor becomes a disgusting mess of excreta and decaying bits of prey. One marvels that babies don't die of infection.

When immatures are of banding size, they are

absolutely charming balls, little clowns made of dense, downy feathers, beak and feet almost hidden in fluff. Beaks snap and click at banders nonstop. Little ones appear to be grapefruit-size, but on feeling them one discovers they are really only lemon-size, so thick the feathering.

Wingspread of these little buffoons is eighteen to twenty-four inches, long for so small a body, but promising great flexibility for hunting. Young fly about twenty-eight days after hatching, meaning faithful parents have been tied down for nearly two months.

Calls are eerie, mournful whinnies, rising and falling in quavery waves. These birds come readily to imitated or recorded calls.

Attracted by a pet canary inside a window, I have seen a screech owl watch it intently, often pecking at the glass in his eagerness to catch this bright morsel.

Because screech owls fly out to catch large insects in air, they are not uncommon victims of automobiles and electric fences. They have a fairly long life; in fact, one was reported to have lived eighteen years.

November 11, 1995

Yank, Yank

THE FIRST TIME YOU watch a white-breasted nuthatch spiral down a tree headfirst, you wonder if you're seeing things. Short legs keep his body close to the trunk. Instead of the suction cups you think he must have on both feet, powerful long, sharp claws give stability for the acrobatics. Observing closely, you may notice that his toes are frequently placed at right angles to his body.

The only other bird that goes headfirst down a tree is the black-and-white warbler, a species that we see here only on migration.

North America has four members of the charming Sittidae family. In Michigan, the white-breasted nuthatch is the most familiar. Short-tailed and short-legged, he's a tubby little slate-blue fellow, well endowed with personality and distinctive idiosyncrasies.

Male and female plumages are similar, except that her bluish back is grayer and her jet black cap is duller, less glossy. Under-tail coverts are light chestnut. In flight, you'll see white patches on tail corners. Male and female nuthatches seem to form a pair bond and stick together year round, keeping your sunflower seed and suet supplies moving briskly.

Tapered black bills are long, given the bird's small size, and are slightly upturned at the end, a design enabling them to poke and pry in and under bark crevices for insects—eggs, larvae, and adults—and spiders. Strong bills are also useful for secreting seeds or nuts in cracks or under loose bark for retrieval later. Nostrils are concealed by bristly tufts, as in woodpeckers.

Of their food habits, Edward H. Forbush, in *Birds of Massachusetts,* wrote:

> Among the pests taken . . . are scale-insects, nut-weevils, locust-seed weevils, leaf-beetles, plant-lice and their eggs, snap-beetles, wood-boring beetles, plants, flies, and eggs of the canker-worm moth. The stomach of one bird taken in my orchard contained 1,629 eggs of the canker-worm moth. The bird eats the hairy larvae of the gipsy moth and the forest tent caterpillar.

Nuthatches's nasal *yank-yank* calls are welcome sounds in woodlands. There are also some light twittering notes too soft for most of us to hear. Henry David Thoreau observed that the song resembled *to what what what what.*

Obligate hole nesters, nuthatches use old woodpecker holes, rotted knotholes, or even one self-excavated in soft decayed wood. Nest holes are lined comfortably with shreds of inner bark, rabbit fur, wool, cow hair, or feathers, in contrast to woodpeckers who use no lining materials.

The Atlas of Breeding Birds of Michigan shows the white-breasted nuthatch present throughout the state and nesting in seventy-five percent of the townships. They are more numerous in the southern Lower Peninsula in a wide range of deciduous habitats. They are found throughout the continental United States, except in the Great Plains. There is movement south in winter, but some are always found here. In winter, they troop the woods with chickadees and downy woodpeckers, making frequent stops at handy bird feeders. Sometimes all will feed in the same tree. At night, they roost alone in a tree cavity.

Nuthatches are well known for being picky at platform feeders, weighing six or eight seeds before finally choosing one. In contrast to blue jays and chickadees, who hold nuts with one foot and crack out the kernel, nuthatches push the food into a crack and hammer out the meat—hatching the nut, as it were.

In October one year, I banded a male nuthatch that showed up July 3d four years later with his tail in bad shape—only one blue-gray feather left and all white-tipped feathers on his left side missing, making flight difficult and uncertain. Number 840-14943 appeared in my net again on September 2d with all feathers renewed. It's always encouraging to know that our woodlands can support a five-inch bird over a long period.

In the spring, opportunistic nuthatches are known

to drink sap from sapsucker wells and to take tufts of fur from a dead squirrel for nest lining.

We once watched a female nuthatch stripping off soft inner bark on the bottom side of a barkless dead black walnut branch. Swift and agile, she made repeated trips in a direct business-like manner, flying off with a billful for nest lining and returning to the supply immediately for another load, over and over.

Resident nuthatches have discovered that I sometimes place cracked nutmeats on a flat railing amid scattered sunflower seeds. One handsome male walks the plank, avoids the seeds, and continues until he reaches the largest nut fragment. He deftly grabs this in his bill and takes off swiftly. He's back so soon I know he hid it, because there wasn't time to break up and eat it. Again, he seeks out the largest piece and takes off—again and again—always selecting the best piece. Only when the nuts are gone will he take a seed.

August 12, 2000

Lawn Patroller

WHEN DOES SPRING begin for you? When a furry pussy-willow emerges from its mahogany colored restraint? With the first cheery whistle of a cardinal high in a treetop on a bright February morning? With pepper and salt in flower at the Kalamazoo Nature Center? For many people it's the sight of a red-red robin bob-bob-bobbin' along. A few redbreasts, seasoned in survival technique may have stayed all winter in sheltered berry-rich lowlands, but the first early wake-up call, *cheerily-cheery-cheer* is always welcome.

There may be snow and cold and raw windy days ahead but *Turdus migratorious* perseveres, starting nesting almost on arrival. Robins head north from winter residences as soon as spring temperatures reach thirty-five degrees when frost is out of the ground and earthworms come up from their winter hideouts below the frostline.

One naturalist friend claims that she knew this bird only as justarobin because that's what her family always said. When she learned how to read, she thought robin was a new bird for her list.

The recent census of breeding birds of Michigan noted that robins were found in every county in the state, in more census blocks than any other species. Even Upper Peninsula and Southern Canada areas find a few overwintering robins, underscoring the strength and adaptability of this species. One expects seed-eaters to stay north in winter, but not those relying on insects, rose hips, holly berries, crabapples, and fruit from mountain ash and autumn olive. How very observant and persistent such survivors must be. Are they brave or don't they know any better?

Robins, unlike many other species, have actually profited by clearing and settling activities because they like neither forests nor fields. They can be found all over North America, high and low, as far north as trees grow. Early in my birding days I was high in the Arizona mountains stalking a good-sized ground bird under ponderosa pines. I was both surprised and disappointed when it turned out to be justarobin. I was seeking something new and different.

A nice way to interest children in robins is to help them learn the male-female difference in plumage. Both have slaty-brown backs and red breasts but she will be duller. Both have broken eye rings—incomplete white spectacles surrounding the eyes. But where the male's head will be bright black—contrasting strongly with the eye ring and back—female heads will be gray. The chin bib is streaked black and white in both.

The young resemble their parents except that they are paler all over and their breasts appear blotchy with large black spots and speckles, a characteristic of all members of the thrush family.

When robins fly, white tail tips show plainly. These spots, known as call-colors, enable birds to see each other and stay together when flying in flocks. Dark feet and legs are strong and sturdy. Albinism—some white feathers—is a quite common condition in robins.

Substantial nests are built in crotches of trees or shrubs, or on man-made shelves and no particular efforts are made to conceal them. Sites from previous years are often used, but a new nest will be built inside the old one if space permits. Rootlets, fine straw, leaves, and grasses are gathered. When a good start at arranging a bowl is complete, a parent seeks a soft mud supply. After many billfuls are laid in place, the robin molds the mud to its body by turning round and round. Before the mud hardens completely, a neat lining of fine grass or rootlets is installed.

Four bluish-green eggs —robin's egg blue—are laid and incubated for about two weeks. Both parents brood and care for them, pressed to the limit by their nestlings' huge appetites.

One professor, experimenting, found that each young robin would take sixty-eight earthworms daily; worms which laid end to end would measure close to fourteen feet. Second broods are common, usually with a new nest being constructed.

Edwin Way Teale's *Wandering Through Winter* tells of "a robin that built its nest in the arm of an active oil pump, and then, after the action resumed, brooded its young and fed its young in a nest that continually rose and fell a yard or more through the air." Another Teale tale was of a robin "nesting in a tree nursery when the tree was dug up and transported twenty miles with the robin still sitting on the eggs."

Because much of their food comes from ground organisms, robins are sensitive to all manner of pesticides, herbicides, and fertilizers. They won't visit over-treated lawns because too many of their food favorites have been killed. Michigan ornithologist George Wallace's data on dead and dying robins on the Michigan State University campus, following DDT spraying for Dutch elm disease, was basic to Rachel Carson's conclusions in *Silent Spring*. Because DDT is still being used outside the United States, migratory passerines are still being exposed to it.

May 31, 1997

19

The Eyes Have It

Eyes in human bodies develop numerous problems as their owners age. Do bird's retinas detach or degenerate? Can a bald eagle at thirty years see as far as he did at the age of five? A soaring eagle can see the form of a crouched cottontail from far away; we would see only the grass. It's as if the raptor had built-in, six power field glasses. Does this long-distance keenness of vision, so vital to survival, deteriorate? I don't suppose we'll ever know, but it's fun to speculate.

Birds can see better than any other animal and learn more about their habitats through their remarkable vision than through all their other senses put together.

Ornithologists and biophysicists spend many hours figuring out how avian eyes work. They've learned that predator species, such as owls, have eyes located toward the front of their heads giving them binocular vision and enabling them to locate, gauge distances, and capture prey, thus making them the successful species that they are. The owl can swivel its flexible neck almost 280 degrees without moving his body, but his eyes are so enormous, jammed into his cranium, that they are almost immovable. His eyes make up fifteen percent of his head's total weight, whereas our eyes are one percent of our head's weight.

If the bird is a quail, a prey species, his eyes will be at the side of his head. He can see almost the entire horizon, to sense dangerous movements, without moving head and body. But he has monocular vision with little overlap and with no sense of distance.

A British ornithologist has said that a man could not thread a needle if he had birds' eyes, but if a bird had a man's eyes, any cat not making a frontal attack could catch him. If you see a robin cocking his head, he may be looking at an object from two different angles in order to estimate distance.

Most of our local owls have yellow or yellow-orange eyes, quite dramatic in all-brown or all-white faces. But our barred owls have brown eyes. Could this yellow coloring give some special advantage?

We know that birds active in the daytime can see color because of their reaction to other birds, in courtship recognition for instance. If an artificial moustache is painted on a female flicker, other flickers will treat her as a male. Nocturnal birds, on the other hand, do not have good color vision cells, but are compensated for this absence by sensitive hearing. Barn owls can catch mice in total darkness.

The lower eyelid of most birds is more flexible than

the upper whereas human eyelids are just the opposite. Snowy owls are frequently photographed when the lower lid is halfway up—their natural position—giving them an odd sleepy look. Eyelids are actually used only when the bird is sleeping, because they have a third one, called the nictitans or nictitating membrane.

Operating like a windshield wiper, the nictitans comes across the eye from the outside corner, not up and down. It is a thin transparent tissue, under the eyelids, which serves to clean and moisten the cornea. The most important function is to protect eyes from drying air currents when the bird is flying—to be the skier's goggles, in a word. With a blink, the membrane protects a woodpecker's eyes from flying chip damage when he's at work chopping wood.

In ducks and loons, the nictitans has a clear window which serves as an underwater contact lens.

Birds, especially owls, have large numbers of rod cells giving them their excellent night vision. A hunting owl can see by starlight what a man sees only during a full moon.

Birds are capable of celestial navigation—seeing and coordinating sun and star data as visual guides—according to ornithologists studying migration. Men need instruments to get where they are going.

July 6, 1996

The Kestrel

THE AMERICAN KESTREL, a feisty little four-ounce falcon, is a permanent resident of Michigan, found in forest openings, marshes, university campuses, cemeteries, grasslands, and agricultural areas. Populations shift south in the winter, but some can be found all year.

Watching a kestrel hover, a habit unique to the falcon family, is an unforgettable treat of bird watching. How can this slender little bird, smaller than a robin, stand on air, just hang there fluttering? Do his long, pointed wings give him extra strength?

Male kestrels have plain rufous-red napes; down their backs this color is barred with black. Inner wings are a warm slate blue and when open they appear black with white spots. The long red tail has a black terminal band and a white tip.

Slightly larger females are browner overall, with more barring, and no blue in the wings. Both sexes have two black mustache marks on white cheeks, although her whiskers are less pronounced.

These birds hunt with rapid wing beats followed by

short glides. A handy field mark, especially helpful when observing from a distance, is their habit of pumping tails up and down after alighting.

Kestrels are commonly seen as they perch on utility wires or posts, surveying the area for the grasshoppers, amphibians, and large invertebrates that are their diet staples. Movement of cars on highways keeps the insects on the move, visible and easily picked off by these hungry falcons.

Sparrow hawk, an old name for the kestrel, is a misnomer because he really feeds chiefly on mice, shrews, voles, frogs, and insects, making him a useful resident of farm fields.

Kestrels swallow small insects whole and hold larger prey with strong sharp talons while tearing it apart with a sharp, curved beak. This raptor obtains eighty percent of his diet from rodents and may eat as many as 290 mice in a single year.

Larger birds of prey were decimated by the presence of accumulated DDT in tissues of the creatures they ate. Because the kestrel's smaller prey did not concentrate DDT in tissues, these populations were not severely affected. Current research indicates that the organo-phosphate fertilizers now in use seem to have a negative effect on this bird's nervous system.

Nests are in natural cavities in earth, buildings, or trees, all holes which have been excavated by someone else. Properly-sized bird houses also are used. They like the same open country that we use for eastern bluebird nest trails. I think you have to choose one species or the other, not provide for both. A hungry kestrel might hassle or even eat a bluebird. If you choose the little predator, mount an appropriate box twelve feet up on pole or tree. Nesting starts in early March. Females lay five brown spotted eggs, incubate them for a month, then brood and feed young in the nest for another month.

Admirers in Iowa have made concerted efforts to provide artificial nest boxes along highways and have had excellent success, the birds seemingly oblivious of passing traffic. A 200-mile trail of boxes reaching from Minnesota to Missouri produces hundreds of nestlings. In the mid 1980s kestrel boxes were placed on the back of traffic signs along Interstate 75 near the Sault in upper Michigan.

In Virginia, Mark Causey monitors seventy-five nests, banding the occupants. Unconcerned about thundering Concordes landing at Dulles Airport, in Washington D.C., these birds live in twenty birdhouses erected by researcher Roger Jones.

You often hear the kestrel before you see him, a high, distinctive *killy-killy-killy*. He calls when excited or alarmed, especially during the courtship period. Although kestrels are protected by law, man is still their greatest enemy. Most banded birds that have been recovered were shot.

November 18, 1995

Yellow-bellied Sapsucker

An always welcome early spring migrant is the yellow-bellied sapsucker. Plumage of this woodpecker family member is well described in Louise Lawrence's superb story of its life called *Mar*.

> Mar is in full nuptial dress. The fine erectile crest feathers glow blood red, matching his scarlet chin patch...a jet-black band spreads across his breast in striking contrast. Black and white geometric lines adorn his head, back, wings, and spiked tail. The veiling of yellowish ochre over his flanks and belly produces a subtle and beautiful counter-shading effect.

The 1994 book, *The Birds of Michigan*, contains John Felsing's splendid sapsucker drawing, showing male and female on a tree trunk beside a pair of black-backed woodpeckers.

Larger than downy woodpeckers but smaller than northern flickers, sapsuckers live and breed in northern deciduous and mixed woods where one can hear their serial cheer notes, an unusual catlike sound. They are quiet on migration but noisy at breeding sites.

An unforgettable habit is their way of drilling rows of holes in tree trunks in search of sap runs and nutritious inner bark plant cells which are called cambium and bast. Their tongues are covered with brushy hairs which pick up sap quickly by capillary action. They are known to drill in at least 275 different native trees. I commonly find characteristic holes in tulip trees. Alexander Skutch reported that, in central Illinois, hickory was preferred to other broad-leaved trees; although sap flow was less profuse, it was ten or eleven percent richer in sugar.

Digging those little wells and letting sap collect means small insects, especially ants, are attracted. The ensuing corpse collection becomes "protein a la sap sauce" for at least thirty-five bird species, who thus profit by the sapsucker's strong bill and cranial muscles. Sapsuckers also feed on fruit and insects, sometimes darting out to flycatch in air.

John Eastman contributed to *The Atlas of Breeding Birds of Michigan* the fact that early returning ruby-throated hummingbirds are almost totally dependent on these sap flows before spring blossoms open and provide nectar.

In southern Michigan, sapsuckers are commonly seen and heard as they migrate through around mid-April. They nest above a line running west from Saginaw Bay to Ludington, going as far north in Canada as hardwood forest grows. In winter, they range through the southern United States and as far south as Panama. In *The Birds of Michigan*, Gail McPeek noted that the maximum total to date seen on state Christmas counts is twenty-nine birds. She also reported "They also seem to like their nest trees close to a lake or stream."

Olin Pettingill's 1974 study of birds at the University of Michigan Biological Station at Douglas Lake reported 17 occupied sapsucker nests: "13 were in live aspens, 1 in a dead aspen, 1 in an elm snag and 2 in unidentified dead trees, at heights from 6 to 60 feet."

Nests, usually located near their closest favorite feeding trees, contain young as early as June 20th and as late as July 22d. Three to five all-white eggs are laid at the bottom of a hole dug by both parents, with males doing the most excavating. When eggs are laid, females incubate them by day for twelve to fourteen days while males take the night shift. Fathers also perform most of the feeding and nest sanitation tasks when babies hatch, a role reversal not commonly found in birds.

Lawrence said parents have long work days, at least 17 hours. They collect and carry to the naked, pulsing nestlings a daily load of 127 meals at the rate of 7½ feedings per hour, per chick. Later, as feathers emerge and nestlings have better temperature control of their bodies, feedings are less frequent but larger. Young take flight after 26 days in the nest, a long period of dependency. Parents feed them for another 10 days.

Immature birds are clamorous, constantly calling for

attention. They differ from the parents in appearance—
no red, just an ashy brown, black, and white pattern.

Including nest-building, incubation, and brooding
periods, the total breeding cycle runs seventy to seventy-
five days. Sapsuckers mate for life; both migrate south
and then find their way back north to the same mate
the following spring.

February 21, 1998

On Woodpeckers

I LOVE WOODPECKERS. If all the bird orders were to disappear except one, I would choose to save the Piciformes. Why? Who knows? It's not a family I knew in a suburban childhood, but one to which I became devoted during bird banding years.

Banders learn that woodpeckers in hand are quiet, compared to titmice whose protesting squawks at being restrained ring through the woods. Their eyes never stop peering and blinking with the same random side-to-side head jerks we see them make on suet feeders. But there's no screaming, no jabbing bills.

I often think that, if I had gotten into ornithology before—instead of after—raising a family, I would have reveled in graduate study on woodpeckers. I might even have gone to Cuba to hunt the great ivory-billed where he was last seen. John James Audubon tells of capturing one of these twenty-one-inch wonders and leaving it in his room while he went to dinner. On return, the cabinetry in the room, to the anger of the innkeeper, was reduced to chips. We find chips, much like those long splinters, where our smaller pileated woodpecker has been digging.

Arthur Cleveland Bent's *Life Histories of North American Woodpeckers* tells of Canadian Indians gladly trading two or even three buckskins for one ivory-billed's bill to be fashioned into a coronet for great warriors. The Bent books on North American birds are composed of reports from all available scholars, resulting in incredibly detailed data, worth browsing by any student.

Ivory-billed woodpeckers have not been seen in the United States for close to fifty years, because the intensive logging of mature coastal forests eliminated their habitat.

The next largest woodpecker, the sixteen-inch pileated, is most apt to be seen in dense woods where he can find old dead trees riddled with large black carpenter ants, his favorite food. Researchers, according to Bent, have found as many as 2,600 ants in a single bird's stomach. The characteristic oval and rectangular holes pileateds drill in tree trunks are evidence of their presence. Look for fresh chips two to three inches long, and listen for echoing *wuck-a-wuck-a-wuck* calls, similar to flickers but louder and funnier. Tuck a little cracked corn in those holes to keep them coming when the ant labyrinth is no longer productive.

When our eighty- to 100-year-old forests were logged off, pileated populations shrank, but there's now some evidence that their recovery parallels forest aging. Their territorial requirements, perhaps covering a mile area, are so large that we can never have many of them. A farm woodlot cannot satisfy a pileated any more than it would a wild turkey or a raven.

In woods, we see evidence of pileateds occasionally—sometimes fresh new chips—but more often the characteristic holes. One evening, a pileated—probably a young of the year—flew into a courtyard window at my residence, knocking himself out. I almost had my hand on him when he came to, took off, flying across the court into another window. Again he eluded me at the last minute. If only I had had something to throw over him so we could enjoy looking at him.

Like all woodpeckers, male and female pileateds are similar; the female's flaming crest is smaller and her moustache is black instead of red. In flight, the large white wing patches and the straight flight pattern are distinctive.

In the north, pileateds nest in hardwoods—maple, elm, yellow birch—often near water. In Florida where I have seen the smaller southern form, holes are drilled in cypress, pine, sycamore, even the palms. Both forms feed on wild berries if ants and beetles are not to be found. Nests are built fifteen to seventy feet up, with forty-five feet the average height. They are not used again, except perhaps as a roosting site, but new holes may be dug in the same tree.

Pileateds share parental responsibilities, brooding eggs and bringing food, often relieving each other at remarkably regular intervals. In Door County, Wisconsin, we saw the relief team alternate at forty-five-minute intervals over and over again, a remarkable experience.

Pileated young are born absolutely bare. Since parents use no soft nesting material, one must always be present to keep the nestlings warm. The young keep up a constant hissing sound when wanting to be fed. The parent feeds the young by regurgitation, standing on his head to do so, because the hole is too small for moving around.

Some people call this bird the log-cock. Not only does it have a loud call, but it also likes to do echoing drumrolls, using an old hollow branch as a sounding board.

During an early January blizzard, a maintenance person was plowing a parking lot and moving snow as fast as possible. Suddenly, a pileated flew over heading northwest. Brave bird to be out and about in such weather!

One of Audubon's most stirring and vigorous plates, done life-size—as he insisted all his representations must be—depicts four pileateds around a lichen covered branch, amid autumn's golden yellow grape leaves and dangling stems of blue fruit. A female at the top is taking off with a caterpillar, a male is pecking at ancient barkless wood and two spectacular males—perhaps young of the year—are busy squabbling, wings and red crests a-flare.

Linneaus, who named this beautiful woodpecker, took pileated from the Latin word *pileum*, or cap. Given this large bird's head being scarlet from bill to nape, the choice of name is a natural.

July 17, 1999

Bark Birds

Bᴀʀᴋ ɪs ᴛʜᴇ ᴛᴏᴜɢʜ ᴄᴏᴠᴇʀɪɴɢ of a woody root or stem, but for various forms of wildlife it does far more than just protect interior fibers. Let's look at some of our winged creatures who could be dubbed "bark birds" because of their dependency on bark, their constant foraging on tree surfaces. Scientists say that bark is a niche for certain species, the specific place occupied, especially in relation to their food source.

Perhaps the brown creeper comes to mind first, because his perennial perambulations round and round as he ascends tree trunks, exploring every crack and crevice for food, are unique. When he nears the top, he flutters down to the base of the next tree, only to circle up that one. Sometimes he takes a short hop backward to take a second look.

Only five inches long, weighing less than one-third ounce, the creeper is equipped with bill and claws perfectly adapted to his lifestyle. The probing bill is slender and deeply curved to help in searching. His toes are curved and sharp, with an unusually long hind claw to help him cling to the bark as he skims along. Speckles and streaks of his plumage are monotone brown and white with no distinctive field marks to interrupt his perfect camouflage pattern. Short legs keep his body close to the tree and a long pointed tail is stiffened at the end to serve as a prop in his spiral climbing.

The creeper's deliberate exploration of trunk and branch yields him a menu of "weevils, leaf hoppers, bugs, aphids, leaf eaters, scale insects, katydid eggs, adult ants, sawflies, moths, caterpillars, cocoons of spiders, pupae of coddling moths, spiders and pseudo-scorpions" according to John K. Terres in *The Audubon Society Encyclopedia of North American Birds.*

This creeper's nesting habits also are related to bark because he builds a hammock of natural materials against a trunk under a loose strip of bark, at about eye level. In one of my early ornithology classes the instructor turned us loose in a small woodland opening, telling us only that a bird's nest was near and visible. Not a single one of us found it, so skillfully camouflaged was it in the natural setting.

Another way a brown creeper uses bark is to find a tree in an out-of-the-way place for his nightly roost. Then he slides in under a loose piece and goes to sleep. Many passerines, notably winter wrens and bluebirds, choose to sleep nestled together in groups, often in a bird house, but the creeper is an individualist all the way.

A second obvious woodland bark bird is the black-

and-white warbler who creeps along tree surfaces in search of insect prey. About the size of a brown creeper, he is striped lengthwise in black and white. His coloring is not so inconspicuous as the creeper, and he doesn't hitch in spurts, just flows along, as happy upside down as right side up. He travels both up and down, not limiting himself to either direction. His bill is thin, but unlike other warblers is slightly curved, the better to eat with. He searches for gypsy moth caterpillars, ants, moths, flies, bugs, even a chain of katydid eggs—all food items to be found in bark interstices by a persistent hunter.

The pine warbler, named for his favorite habitat, deliberately creeps over trunk and branch, but also flies out to pick off passing insects. His diet consists primarily of beetles, cotton boll weevils, grasshoppers, and spiders but he takes tree seeds, berries, and grapes on occasion.

Both of these warblers usually fly farther north to nest, but southern Michigan birdwatchers see them on migration.

White-breasted nuthatches are dependent on bark in two ways. First, they are climbers, or rather descenders, since they're famous for coming down tree trunks head first. With very short legs, hanging on only by their thick, sharp curved claws, not bracing with stiffened tail like the creeper, they move down in straight trips, foraging as they go, looking for insects, eggs, or larvae that up-the-trunk creepers with different views might have missed. No other bird travels so consistently in a head-down position.

Secondly, when whitey has a seed that is too large for his bill to handle, he hunts for a fissure, wedges in the seed, then cracks it open, using the bark as a vise, and the bill as a spear.

The smaller red-breasted nuthatch is also an acrobat. He moves over bark, over branches, and around twigs, gleaning rapidly as he goes, and winding as he pleases. He, too, uses bark as a vise to immobilize seeds.

Black-capped chickadees and tufted titmice both use branches as pounding platforms for opening seeds. They hold the seed with their toes and whack away. The chickadee hammers so fast and fiercely one wonders why he doesn't miss and hit a toe. Both birds casually search bark for insect food, but not with the same nonstop, no nonsense diligence characteristic of brown creepers. They move about the branches nimbly, hanging upside down if needed to get a better look.

When the ground was snow covered on Thanksgiving Day, we watched a dark-eyed junco glean under the thistle feeder, then fly up in a maple and busily give three or four sections of bark a good going-over with his bill, much as a chickadee would. This seemed unusual behavior for a ground feeder, but food was clearly the immediate and vital goal.

While doing their brisk ballet dances up, down, and

around branch tips, kinglets search out hibernating insects and spider egg sacs, while flicking their wings and hovering here and there, always in movement.

All woodpeckers are tree dependent as evident in their name. The yellow-bellied sapsucker drills holes through tough outer bark to get at his favorite soft inner bark, and especially to lap up sap that fills the shallow holes and soon attracts insects.

In *Mar*, Lawrence tells us that these birds have found another use for rough-barked trees. In order to maintain nest sanitation, when adults remove the neatly sealed membranous sacs which their young excrete, they carefully deposit them in a crevice in the bark. Parents decorate the same tree with fecal sacs for the four weeks young are in the nest.

Hal Harrison's *A Field Guide to Birds' Nests* gives detailed descriptions of the various materials different birds use in nest construction. He sites an amazing 57 species who use bark in some form: 16 species use strips; 8, fibers; 7, shreds; 7, fine bark; 5, inner strips; 3, large strips; 2, inner bark; 1, papery bark. The Baltimore oriole, blue-winged warbler, and black-and-white warbler specify grapevine bark; and the American redstart and Philadelphia vireo want birch bark.

Doesn't it make you wonder how birds distinguish one tree species from another? Doesn't it make you want to go on a tree-planting binge in the spring to help birds satisfy their idiosyncratic tastes?

January 4, 1997

Piggyback on Mom or Dad

An unusual, always welcome April delight, is to spot a common loon on one of the many small glacial pothole lakes that dot the countryside. Once in a great while, a red-throated loon is seen in Michigan in winter on a bit of open water. I have, however, seen one only in the Pacific Ocean off British Columbia.

Common loons generally winter on saltwater along both coasts, but raise their young in secluded freshwater lakes where there is no high-speed boating activity. Their nests, along the water's edge, protected from wave action and wind, are made of piled-up earth and packed-down moss, twigs, grasses, and reeds. Prefab ones may be found on top of old muskrat houses. Construction is a long-term major project continuing throughout the incubation period.

Loons are large, heavy-bodied birds, twenty-eight to thirty-five inches long—a foot longer than a mallard—and need large nests. One parent is on the nest protecting eggs ninety-nine percent of the time during the four weeks of incubation. That's a lot of sitting, and explains the necessity of locating it in a quiet out-of-the-way place.

As human populations, urban sprawl, commercial fishing, shoreline development, marinas, and recreational boating increased in Michigan, nesting areas moved steadily northward. Now we see common loons only as they move back and forth from winter feeding areas around the Florida coast, proven by the finding of our Michigan bands on Florida loons. A rare few nest in a southwest county.

Birds of solitary habits, loons especially like islands or bog mats for breeding sites because they are safe from prowling land predators. The same site may be used year after year. In his 1975 work, Harrison wrote that six of eight man-made platforms in Minnesota were accepted for nests. Oval, greenish-brown eggs are thick-shelled, the size of those of geese. Incubation starts as soon as one egg has been laid. Only one brood a season is possible.

Observing courtship rituals is a rare privilege because they involve dramatic chases, ceremonial bill-dipping, and an amazing amount of tremulous wailing.

One reason why the future existence of these birds remains precarious is the fact that they don't have large broods like ducks and geese. Just one or two eggs is the rule. I remember a group of us walking into a Door County nature center years ago and enthusiastically telling the naturalist about the large flock of loon chicks with parents we'd just seen out on the lake. "Couldn't be," he said. "Never more than two." Crestfallen, we went back to the field guides again. So learning occurs.

The movie *On Golden Pond* featured the distinctive eerie calls of the common loon. Their yodel is heard most often in breeding areas and is one of the true wilderness sounds of the north woods. Some tapes of the mournful tremolo call and the undulating yodel are good and delightful to play, so evocative of wildness. But there's nothing like hearing the real thing as you hike near a lake in Michigan's Upper Peninsula.

In *Naming Nature*, naturalist Mary Blocksma wrote of the loon's unearthly laughter: "some wild place in my heart laughs back."

A word as to plumage: a black and white checkered back and a striped necklace provide accent to the heavy, all-black head and stout black bill. The eye is dark ruby. Sexes are alike. In good light, head feathers show a greenish or purplish iridescence.

Winter and juvenile plumages do not feature the checkerboard, but are dark above with white underparts. When adults molt twice a year, all flight feathers are shed simultaneously, making for flightlessness. Full adult plumage is attained by about twenty-five months.

Any disturbance during the mating season means nest abandonment and failure. Once hatched, little sooty-black down puffs ride around on parents' backs until they are able to venture or fish on their own.

Sibling rivalry, strong in loons, often results in the death of one chick from fierce pecking by sister or brother. Juveniles need the entire summer to gain sufficient size and strength to migrate, which means that parents often go south first, leaving children to find their own path down uncharted ways, another of nature's unfathomable miracles. The young often stay south until the second spring, when they return north to breed.

Referring to loon's intelligence, naturalist Teale told of watching six of them far out on a northern Maine lake when a blue jay gave his alarm call on the shore. All six heads turned immediately in its direction.

Bird books list a dozen fish species that are diet specialties, along with shrimp, frogs, snails, and insects. But a friend of ecologist Richard Brewer watched a loon catching and eating young ducklings in the summer of 1995.

Their feet have three front toes, fully webbed and ending in sharp nails. The small hind toe has a flap, but is not webbed. Legs, though powerful, are short and placed at the rear end of the body, making the birds awkward on land. They are great divers and fast fliers, but poor walkers.

Because the birds are heavy, eight or nine pounds, they must patter across the water for some distance, even as much as one-fourth mile to become airborne. Lakes chosen for breeding must be large enough to permit this long preflight, and deep enough for escape-diving if being pursued. In flight, the species has a distinctive humpbacked posture, characteristic of all members of this family.

Water birds, such as loons and pied-billed grebes, are surface divers, getting momentum from a quick, powerful forward leap. They vanish, only to emerge some time later, many yards away. They also have a unique ability to release the air out of sacks in their bodies, submerging gradually, and then floating along, with heads just above the water like a submarine with its periscope tip barely showing. When the water is the least bit rough, it's almost impossible for eager bird watchers to figure out what those dark bumps are.

My most memorable loon experience, a sad and curious one, occurred at Michigan's Wilderness State Park. Walking along water's edge, I found a feathered carcass of an emaciated common loon with the skeleton of a snake hanging from his bill. How I would have loved to witness that encounter. Who killed whom, and how? Did the bird die of starvation because it couldn't catch a fish? Or…?

The Whitefish Point Bird Observatory area, at the northeast corner of the U.P., is a good place to see loons in early May as migrants pass into Canada across the narrowest part of Lake Superior. Because they are day rather than night fliers, as many as a thousand may be seen in one day.

Michigan researchers in the Seney area found that

the easiest way to catch birds needed for lead and mercury poison monitoring is to use a boat at night with a light and a large net, because loons usually sleep on the water. Blood samples can be obtained and the bird released immediately. In *Loon Call*, Dave Evers reported that observations of 800 color-marked birds show high site fidelity between years, but with frequent nest switching.

As to longevity, a loon banded in Ontario, found in New Jersey, was seven and one half years old.

Common loons were designated a threatened species by the Michigan legislature in 1987. At that time, the Michigan Loon Preservation Association was formed. Recent estimates indicate about 300 breeding pairs in the state, with more than half of these north of the Mackinac Bridge.

May 10, 1997

Are You a Birdscaper?

H<small>AVE YOU EVER THOUGHT SERIOUSLY</small> about making your yard more attractive to birds? What birds do you see now? Which ones might it be possible to see? Even minor changes in the trees and shrubs you plant can make a big difference in your visitor list. Be sure your fall plantings include some treats for them.

Think for a minute about what is needed for safety and comfort. As humans, we need food, shelter, and clothing. Birds come to us beautifully clothed, but we can increase the opportunities for food and shelter. Their dietary tastes are specific. Some want seeds, many choose insects especially for their nestlings, some like fruit, and a few need nectar, pollen, or even petals. Every spring, house sparrows eat our yellow crocus petals yet never bother the purple or white ones.

A basic principle in planning a bird sanctuary is to maximize the diversity of your offerings. Have as many species of trees, shrubs, and flowers as possible. And try to have lots of them be native species. Native birds will often find native plants—their old friends—more attractive than imports. As our concern increases for the inroads that human population pressures are putting on the natural world, various people and groups are working to protect the existence and diversity of our native flora. Across Michigan, dozens of nurseries are increasing their offerings of native trees, shrubs, and flowers. Some will help you make choices suitable for your purse and for the size and nature of your land. Is it a city lot or an apartment deck, an upland prairie, a wetland, or a woodland acreage?

Mix evergreen and deciduous woody types. A diversity of offerings may boost your guest list. Keep the area, whether small or large, as wild as possible given your location and preferences. Use more native ground covers such as wild ginger or bearberry to reduce sterile lawn areas. Designing flowerbed edges in an irregular pattern is a good idea. Use a garden hose to help you choose and define a free-flowing pattern. Birds need sheltering shrubs and low branches, but they like open areas near thickets for feeding, so maintain both sun and shade. The thickets provide shelter from foul weather and predators. A lawn that hasn't been neutralized by insecticides or herbicides will harbor more ants, crickets, grasshoppers, grubs, and beetles—those proteins so important for stuffing in baby birds' mouths.

White pine, Michigan's state tree, provides both nesting sites and roosting cover. Such shelter is critical on stormy nights. But it grows very large very quickly, and you may want to consider smaller evergreens such as yew, red or white cedar, or low-growing junipers. Woody plants with winter berries are an important choice for winter residents and for hungry spring migrants on their way north. A flock of cedar waxwings will find rest and refreshment in your hawthorn stand.

Checklists of trees and shrubs attractive to birds are long and varied and generously sprinkled with such reliables as cherry, maple, willow, and crabapple. If you need short-term results in small spaces, try vines. Use shadbush, holly, even mulberry if it won't be shedding fruit on sidewalks or driveways. Planting older, larger trees brings results soon, but is more expensive and labor intensive. Pin oak and red maple are dependable, fast growing towering natives. Stately tulip trees provide nectar for hummers and seed for cardinals.

Many folk opt for shrubs because of their wide availability, low cost, fast growth, and variety of seeds and berries. Some long-term favorites such as dogwood and mountain ash are threatened with disease, so consult your friendly nursery and helpful catalogs.

Living fences of roses, barberries, or blueberries can increase your privacy while offering nesting sites and a feeding smorgasbord. Don't be neat. Leave seeds on your zinnias. Let grasses and weeds grow behind the garage; keep a big brush pile, a busy corner. Leave some leaves under bushes and some dead branches on trees.

May 6, 2000

Meow

Do you have a gray catbird nesting in a tangle? More often heard than seen, they are common nesters and are also found here casually between October and mid-April. I remember a local bird enthusiast finding one in a dense swampy area on a Dowagiac Christmas count, my only December record ever.

They are sleek, long-tailed, well tailored, slate-gray birds that sport a trim black cap, with no sexual or seasonal differences in plumage. The most noticeable field marks, if you have the bird in hand, are the rusty under-tail coverts, flaunted only in courtship display. He wears his red flannels all year long.

The petulant call note that gives them their name is a whining *meow*, often revealing their presence. Like mockingbirds, they are known to mimic other birds—from cardinals to chickens—the reason for their group name of mimic thrushes.

The run-on soft, disjointed, somewhat melodic song is interspersed with pauses, chucks, and strident scolds, but a distinctive *meow* always creeps in. It is written that the true song of a catbird, given in early mornings, is beautiful. He may sing exposed on a fence or porch railing or hidden in his thorny thicket. Naturalist Jim Granlund has observed that its repertoire of songs increases with age.

Inhabitants of dense, bushy lowlands, catbirds nest in the thickest part of shrubby tangles; usually placing their well hidden nests below ten feet. Twigs and leaves are main construction materials with bark shreds and soft rootlets used for lining. Four to six dark greenish–blue eggs are usual, and two broods are common. Catbirds are known to recognize and reject cowbird eggs. Nests, although bulky and untidy, are sufficiently sturdy that other birds and small rodents reuse them as storage and feeding platforms.

Small insects—ants, beetle, grasshoppers—and spiders are chief menu items, especially for feeding young. Many injurious insects go down baby throats. One study showed that sixty-two percent of youngsters' food consisted of cutworms. Later in the season, fruits and berries, especially elderberries and mulberries, are staple foods.

Catbirds are at ease with humans, often living near habitations, nesting in berry bush thickets or overgrown grapevines on the garden fence. (Keep your cats in the house.)

Fond of water and bathing, these birds spend a long

time splashing and preening, and finally sunbathing. No wonder they look so neat and trim as they flit around nervously, tilting and twitching long tails.

Catbirds are found throughout Michigan, with heavier concentrations in the southwest corner. Michigan breeding bird census data reported two birds on most Upper Peninsula routes and as many as 14 on routes in our area. In my 55-acre woodland research tract in the Indiana dunes, I recorded 54 nestings in 12 years. The species nests throughout most of the United States, although in small numbers in the southwest and mountain west.

Most migrate to southern states or Central America, often flying directly over the Gulf of Mexico, resting on small islands as needed.

Bird banding records show catbirds living as long as ten years and four months, but two to four years is probably a more common life span.

September 9, 2000

The Carolina Wren

IF A LOUD, CLEAR *teakettle, teakettle, teakettle tee* or *wheedle, wheedle, wheedle* rings through your woods, grab your 'nocs and go looking, because it has to be made by a Carolina wren.

At six inches, the largest of our eastern wrens, *Thryothorus ludovicianus* is rusty brown with white chin and buff underparts. A conspicuous white eyeline, narrowly bordered above by black, is distinctive all through the year.

The downward curved bill and long rufous tail, finely barred with black, and often cocked over the back, will confirm your sighting. Carolina wrens are one of those obliging species with minimal age, sex, and seasonal differences in feathering.

Another obliging habit of this LBJ (little brown job) is that, according to the dean of bird song scholars, Aretas Saunders, this bird sings "more or less throughout the year," whereas most species sing only in the breeding season. A silent, snowy winter woods becomes alive when *teakettle, teakettle* rings out.

In his 1979 summary of Kalamazoo area birds, Raymond J. Adams, Jr., research director of the Kalamazoo Nature Center, graphed the Carolina wren as an uncommon, permanent resident. There have been ups and downs in the population because of this essentially southern bird's sensitivity to cold. To quote Charles Nelson from *The Birds of Michigan*: "The worst crash in recent years came with the harsh winters of the late 1970s when the entire Michigan population was wiped out." There has been a slow, steady comeback. In Michigan, the northern edge of the Carolina's range, is found in the lower three tiers of counties.

In the 1997 edition of *Birds of the Indiana Dunes*, Kenneth J. Brock wrote: "The hard winters of 1976-77 and 1977-78 decimated the Carolina wren population. By 1990 numbers had rebounded, but decreased again following the winter of 1993-94."

Its melodious call is so cheerful, so commanding, the activity so constant, and the bird so seemingly curious, that one is immediately charmed, even more than with other members of the Troglodytidae family.

The dictionary defines a troglodyte as a member of a primitive people living in caves and—especially—an unsocial, reclusive person. The first part of the definition fits because all wrens nest in holes or secluded spots. The unsocial, reclusive phrase absolutely does not apply. True, we hear one more often than we see one, but only because it's so busy exploring greenbrier tangles or dense brush piles that we're not quick enough to spot it.

One late October day, we were walking the swampy part of a woods when one of these curious, cheerful bits of feather energetically investigated us from a sumac top, calling again and again. Such a wild lowland tangle devoid of human intrusion would be paradise for this habitué of damp undergrowth. Tiny winter wrens, who summer farther north, feed and nest in similar habitats.

Carolina wren's legs are long for the bird's overall size, giving good leverage to peck and poke in dark crevices and corners. Roots of upturned trees along stream banks are favorite feeding and nesting sites.

My Chester A. Reed beat-up limp leather bound 1895 *Handbook of Birds* says: "Whatever he may be when he is alone, he is never at rest as long as he imagines himself observed. Now he is on this side of us, now on that; a moment later on a stump before us, bobbing up and down and gesticulating wildly with his expressive tail."

Teale tells of Carolina wrens nesting in "pockets of old coats hanging in sheds." A friend who lived along the Mississippi River, in northern Illinois, told me of hearing chirps in her basement regularly but she couldn't find the maker. Nut-cracking leavings left on the bench were thoroughly gleaned. But how did this bird get in? She puzzled over this for several winters before finally discovering a small round hole left by a long-ago water pipe. A rose tangle outside and littered tool bench inside obscured comings and goings.

In 1998 a Carolina wren built a nest into a twenty-four-inch spruce holiday wreath still hanging on a friend's seldom-used front door. All writers say these birds build well-concealed nests made of a variety of materials: grasses, inner bark strips, weed stalks, feathers, discarded snakeskin pieces. There is even a record of one made mostly of hairpins. Nests are often domed or roofed over.

Our bird had read the ornithology texts and built accordingly. The almost invisible nest, intricately woven of white pine needles, lots of moss, faded grasses, plant down from sweet everlasting, and small oak leaves had a few eight inch-long twigs protruding. The nest pocket was tucked down between two of the three large pine cones. Five eggs were laid, but when the nest was vandalized, perhaps by a blue jay, the young were thrown out and lost. The resident is happy to report that Carolina wrens were again in evidence in January 1999.

In winter, Carolinas feed on fruits of poison ivy, bayberry, pine, oak, and sweet gum. The balance of the year, ants are preferred food followed by flies, millipedes, cotton boll weevils, cockroaches, caterpillars, sow bugs, crickets, snails, moths, and small vertebrate animals.

In Forbush's 1929 third volume of *Birds of Massachusetts* he informs us that Carolina wrens enjoyed his feeder specialties: ground peanuts, suet, marrow from a marrow bone, and hamburger steak. Another author, who provided chopped cheese, said the Carolina would hop up on his door frame when the cupboard was bare. The same author reports that a Carolina is "skittish at the bath, buzzes at the surface of the water and instantly buzzes off to flutter violently, as if drenched."

Because of their innate curiosity, Carolina wrens respond well to your pishing call or to the sound made by kissing the back of your hand. If you hear *teakettle, teakettle* near your house, try some pishing and watch to see who answers.

April 17 and 24, 1999

A Natty Dresser

TUFTED TITMICE ARE FAMILIAR permanent resident birds who troop our woodlands with chickadees, nuthatches, and downy woodpeckers. On a snowy, cold December day our Audubon hikers found members of this group together, gleaning bark crevices in tree tops just as if they hadn't already been over those same trees five times before. They must eat the equivalent of thirty percent of their body's weight daily in order to survive.

Titmice have made a major range expansion northward during the last century, partly the result of an increase in winter bird feeding, but also because of climatic warming and reforestation of abandoned farmland. In Michigan, they now nest in every county in the southern part of the Lower Peninsula, with only a few breeding farther north. First recorded in the state in 1879, their range lies east of the Great Plains and south of the Great Lakes. Bridled and plain titmice, close *Parus* genus cousins, live in the dry Southwest.

The titmouse is characterized by soft, fluffy, slate-gray plumage and a nicely rounded tail. Brownish or rusty feathers on sides and flanks are more apparent in winter. There are no marked seasonal, age, or sex plumage differences. Erect, pointed gray crests, which can be raised or lowered at will, are conspicuous above black forehead feathers. Faces are white, eyes are large and black, enhanced by a black spot directly above them, giving a wide-eyed look of perpetual surprise. Legs are longer than chickadees or nuthatches.

The short, conical, black bills are unnotched, lacking side bristles characteristic of birds who pursue flying insects. Some stiff hairs conceal nostrils at the bill's base.

Titmice are energetic, not quite so active or acrobatic as chickadees, continually flitting in and out of feeders quickly, taking the chosen sunflower seed to a nearby branch where they wedge it under a foot, pecking between toes to hack out the kernel with their sharp bill. Tails are weak and not used as support in climbing as a brown creeper's does.

Their diet is two-thirds animal food, consisting of caterpillars, beetles, bees, wasps, ants, larvae, treehoppers, insect eggs, and often spiders, in season. The vegetable food eaten in fall and winter includes berries, wild cherries, sumac and tulip seeds, also soft-shelled nuts from oak and beech trees. Titmice are fond of sunflower seeds and will take suet and broken bread pieces from feeders.

Arrival at the feeder is often announced by a clear

ringing *peter, peter, peter* call, a sound large for the size of the bird. Birds of both sexes sing, but the female less frequently. In hand, banders find titmice feisty, constantly jabbing at the restraining hand, not biting, but pecking hard repeatedly and scolding loud enough to call in every bird in the neighborhood.

Audubon, in his superb collection of drawings from *Birds of America*, portrayed a pair of titmice busily feeding in a pine tree, both birds totally intent on finding delectable morsels. One bird is in the characteristic head-upside-down position inspecting a branch tip.

Birds of no known bad habits, tufted titmice are curious. They respond to a whistle, seeming tame and confiding to observers. In his unbelievably complete 1,109 page tome, *The Audubon Society Encyclopedia of North American Birds*, Terres wrote of the titmouse,

. . .tame, comes near at sound of human voices, intelligent, quick to learn, takes food from one's hands, quickly stores sunflower seeds in bark crevices or in ground, responds to squeaking, imitations of its calls bring it near with remarkable boldness.

Prolific breeders, titmice must have a cavity for their nest, so breeding success depends on the presence of dead trees in which they can excavate holes. Ornithologists classify them as "obligate hole nesters," reminding us of our responsibility to leave standing dead trees in woodlands. They also use nesting boxes, bird houses, or abandoned woodpecker holes. In *The Atlas of*

Breeding Birds of Michigan, naturalist John Eastman wrote that a titmouse constructs a nest of "mosses, bark strips, dried grasses, and damp leaves—plus fur, string, and often snakeskins." Both sexes build the nest and she broods the eggs, surviving on food he brings to her. Eggs are white or buff, sprinkled with reddish-brown and a few lavender spots. One good thing about being a cavity nester is that parasitic cowbirds usually leave hole-nesters alone.

Like chickadees, titmouse parents, who mate for life, are quiet and retiring during the nesting season, almost invisible. They have large broods, usually six babies.

The titmouse family I watched during one summer nested in a bluebird box right by a garage, one in which a flying or red squirrel had gnawed the hole larger, making it big enough for titmice. The five babies were as chubby and content as any nestlings I have ever banded, black eyes bright and sparkling. The parents had been constantly in and out of the feeder fifty feet away, and the results of their efforts were apparent in their well-nourished offspring.

Fifty years ago, in *Modern Bird Study*, Ludlow Griscom, then dean of American ornithologists, wrote of the intense and constant busyness of titmice, their constant expenditure of physical energy:

> The price that these small birds pay for this type of physical activity is that they are very short-lived; they burn themselves out, so to speak, in a comparatively brief span

of years. Less active birds, of the less specialized orders, of greater antiquity, with lower body temperatures, live much longer.

Eastman's *The Book of Forest and Thicket* states that the longevity record of titmice is thirteen years. My northern Indiana banding records suggest three to five years as average for wild birds. Whatever their age, titmice are charming, active, vocal members of our year-round avian community.

June 20 and 27, 1998

Brown-headed Cowbirds

Squeaky, unmusical gurgles from a treetop tell us that brown-headed cowbirds have returned from their winter sojourns with friends in Louisiana rice fields. The estimated average winter population in just one parish, between 1974 and 1992, was 9,274,858 birds. Mechanical rice harvesting techniques make large amounts of food readily available.

These birds are brood parasites, having no nest-building instinct and making none of their own. Their speckled eggs have been found in nests of more than 200 species. They pose serious threats to the well-being of birds they parasitize, especially if the populations of targeted species are small.

The cowbird's range includes all forty-eight contiguous states and Canada, with major breeding areas concentrated in the middle west and southern California. Bronzed cowbird dominates much of the southwest. Since 1988, the South American and West Indies species, shiny cowbird, has been recorded in Florida which had not previously experienced brood parasitism.

Feeding and courtship activities take place in open grassland or agricultural areas, often around cattle feed-lots, dairies, and grain fields located near forests.

The female lays eggs in early morning, sneaking in and completing her swift act within ten seconds. She usually selects nests in forest edges or young clear-cuts. Her eggs have a short incubation period. Nestlings are two or three days old when their tiny nest-mates hatch. The larger young are in a good position to get most the food offered, thus starving the smaller ones. Also, baby cowbirds eject both eggs and chicks out of nests with a deft shouldering motion.

In Indiana, researchers studied 1,340 parasitized nests of more than twenty species, including the red-eyed vireo, worm-eating warbler, ovenbird, and Acadian flycatcher.

Some species of birds seem to sense presence of alien eggs and respond in various ways. One or two, notably the yellow warbler, build a new bottom layer covering all eggs; some, such as warbling vireo and Baltimore oriole, spear an egg or break it into pieces; field sparrows simply desert the nest. Unfortunately, most victims are not aware of the alien presence and suffer grievously, brooding the egg and caring for the oversized fledgling.

If you've once seen a brave little blue-winged warbler, seeming to shrink in fear, but gamely stuffing the mouth of a large newly fledged cowbird, you never forget it. And herein lies the sorrow for many of our neotropical populations, already reduced and threatened by habitat disturbance on both summer and wintering grounds.

At a national workshop on this type of parasitism, Scott Robinson said the problem in Illinois forests is so severe for wood thrushes that they are truly raising only cowbirds. "Multiple parasitism was the rule rather than the exception for many larger host species such as thrushes and tanagers."

One researcher found that giving captive cowbirds a limited amount of calcium supplement significantly reduced fecundity. Also, he reported: "One female cowbird laid seventy-seven eggs, including an egg each day for sixty-seven days, surpassing the previous record for number of eggs produced in a single breeding season by a wild bird."

Kirtland's warbler, Michigan's endangered darling, was so seriously threatened by cowbirds, with seventy percent of the nests parasitized, that controls were initiated in 1972. With increases in amount of suitable Kirtland's habitat after burn areas matured and after cowbird control was instituted, there has been immediate dramatic increase in their population. Maintenance of their population will entail continued costly controls.

Other species with small populations, severely threatened by cowbird parasitism, include the black-headed grosbeak, California gnatcatcher, willow and Acadian flycatchers, hooded warbler, grasshopper sparrow, golden-cheeked warbler, and black-capped, Bell's, gray, and warbling vireos.

June 21, 1997

Wood Warblers

WOOD WARBLERS ARE ONE of the most active, most colorful, and most fascinating of all North American bird groups. They have been the subjects of many research projects and long books. Just their descriptive names—ranging from blackburnian to yellow-throated—may set warbler watchers' pulses racing.

These charmers are under six inches in length with thin, sharp bills suitable for catching such small insects as spruce budworms, blackflies, mosquito larvae, and tiny midges, all of which fuel their energetic life style.

Because molting from beautiful, usually distinctive spring plumage to dull and sombre fall attire makes warbler identification a challenge for even the most experienced birders, becoming comfortably familiar with them can take several years. In southwest Michigan, theoretically, we can see thirty-five of the fifty-seven North American warbler species, but only one-third of these nest here; the balance migrate through in spring and fall, perhaps with stopovers, perhaps not, depending on weather and food supplies.

All birders remember, with a thrill of pleasure, special sightings of certain warblers. On migration, we may find them from ground level up into tree canopies. A glimpse of a black-throated blue gleaning on a sycamore tree or an upside-down black-and-white calmly traversing the underside of a long branch is filed away to be reenjoyed many times.

Imagine our surprise in mid-June 1994, seven degrees above the Arctic Circle at the very top of Baffin Island (get out your atlas), to find a northern waterthrush merrily singing away where a little half-frozen stream entered ice-filled Eclipse Sound. Granted, waterthrushes occasionally nest that far north in Alaska, but the eastern Arctic is cold, barren, rocky and windswept compared to the lushness of Alaskan valleys. How did he get there and how did he fare so far out of his normal range?

Long-term population trends of all neotropical migrants, especially warblers, are dropping dramatically because of hemisphere-wide habitat alterations. We're fragmenting both northern breeding areas and local stopovers. At the end of their southward journey, birds find forests destroyed to increase open land for farming. Human density pressures are multiplying birds' existence problems.

The Michigan Nature Conservancy chapter is conducting research along the northern Lake Huron shoreline, evaluating food habits of both migrant and breeding birds in relation to shoreline development. They are also checking midges, yellow perch, deer, evergreen species, and local economies as contributing parts of the whole picture. This hard-core research is essential to land use decisions that may help slow sharp declines in bird populations.

Kalamazoo area bird banders often have good opportunities to study warblers in hand. The early 1996 season was a difficult one with an extremely late spring and only three inches of rain from mid-June to the end of August. Insects were scarce. Frog and toad surveys seemed like disasters. Scarlet tanagers, eastern phoebes, and brown thrashers set up territories and left. Raccoons had few frogs to eat so they ate bird nestlings instead.

But it turned out to be a banner banding year after all. The 1996 autumn season saw all-time highs of some warbler species, particularly of the Tennessees: 894 banded against a 1990 to 1996 average of 332. And there were 342 Nashvilles compared with an average of 161 during the same period. Both species had stopped locally en route to their central America and northern South America destinations. Perhaps there was an especially successful breeding season in the northern U.S. and Canadian wilds where they had summered, coupled, apparently, with an abundant fall insect supply.

Overall, of twenty-nine species banded, eleven had their highest counts in this decade. Sadly, in contrast, the yellow-rumped warbler 1996 figure was only 235 compared with a 1990 to 1996 average of 1,000 per year. Golden- and ruby-crowned kinglets, even tinier than warblers, were in distressingly low numbers. Did that reflect low populations of insects available to these birds passing through in April? Thrushes too, including my lifelong first love, the wood thrush, were in bad shape: a total of 384 bandings against an average of 687.

But the high warbler counts had banders cheering. One volunteer, who has spent many hours banding hawks at Michigan's Whitefish Point Bird Observatory, is admittedly addicted to these small songsters. After banding two pine warblers, his first ever, he said, "I'd band seven days a week year round if there were warblers available."

August 16, 1997

Brood Patches

Have you heard of a brood patch, also known as an incubation patch? It is one of the amazing facets of bird life, one which most people never have a chance to see.

One of the privileges of being a bird bander is that closeup and personal handling of birds gives unparalleled opportunity for observation, increasing understanding and admiration of the miracle called a bird.

An incubation, or brood patch, is a bare area on the underside of an adult bird where all down feathers have dropped out, allowing the parent to incubate eggs more efficiently. The bared skin becomes coarse, thickened, and spongy, often slightly swollen. Extra veins develop just under the skin, increasing circulation of blood, and therefore generating more heat to support proper development of the embryo.

Brood patches develop only in the sex which incubates the egg: both sexes in woodpeckers and rose-breasted grosbeaks, the female in most song birds, and the male in the phalaropes. Development is initiated by hormonal activity, but does not occur in all feathered species. In penguins, for instance, the egg nestles on top of the male's feet, protected from Antarctic cold by a fold of belly skin. Cormorants, boobies, and frigate birds wrap their large, webbed feet around the eggs to transfer heat.

You've often seen a robin go into her nest, wriggle and squirm as she settles down. She is simply pushing aside the long, protective feathers of breast and flank which hide the brood patch, so that her skin surface may touch each egg. Sometimes she will turn the eggs with her bill to distribute heat evenly.

These brood patches are not visible unless you hold the bird in hand and carefully blow apart the side feathers to expose the bare area.

When the incubation period is over and the young fledge, enlarged veins shrink and skin texture gradually returns to normal. Down feathers grow in slowly and regrowth is completed in subsequent molts.

As with all other avian processes, variations in this chain of events are many, and most interesting to observe. In the spring, bird banders are amazed at the variety in size, location, shape, texture, and venation of brood patches.

Let's look, for example, at breeding habits of downy woodpeckers. The downy is an inhabitant of old woods, the smallest, and for most of us, the most common member of the Picidae. In the first year, young birds of either sex may have red feathers on their crowns. Adult males have a red nape patch, and adult females, except old ones, have no red anywhere. Downies nest in holes in dead trees or branches, and lay pure white eggs on the bare floor. Camouflage egg coloring is not necessary for hole nesters.

Because both downy parents perform nest responsibilities, both develop a bare belly surface. The ugly nestlings are born totally naked; only a mother could love them. Not only must eggs be incubated and adequate food for the parents found, but later, nestlings must be brooded continuously until feather covering and internal heat regulators develop.

Harried parents must also serve as sanitation engineers, an important function for a species whose young stay in the nest as long as twenty-one days. Their bills crammed with high protein soft insects, parents come in and feed their young. The adults depart with white semisoft fecal sacs in their bills, discarding them at a safe distance from the nest, often over water. Adults may eat the fecal sac because the young don't fully digest their food and busy parents need every calorie available.

Banding data from one ten-year period shows handling of downies on seventy-nine occasions. Here are samples of some spring entries which convey the varied wonders of the brood patch development:

April 5	Female	Small clear area—just starting.
May 7	Female	Large clear area—lower abdominal bulge—egg?
June 19	Female	Clear from top to bottom—¾ x 1 ¾ inches. Extra veins on swollen lower abdomen.
May 21	Male	Clear area—¾ x 1 ¼ inches.
June 3	Male	Huge clear area. Wrinkles not engorged.
June 12	Male	Patch clear—¾ x 1 ½ inches.

In the case of current year downies, too young to be nesting, there is often a completely clear pink breast area with smooth surface and no venous development. Is this a case of what we learned in high school biology sixty years ago: ontogeny recapitulates phylogeny?

One June, a friend brought me a dead female hummingbird. Even this tiny creature's underside was amazingly bare, the better to disseminate heat to her two pea-sized eggs.

With this introduction to the whys and wherefores of bird reproduction, one can see that there is an exciting process going on hidden from our sight.

July 12, 1997

How Do They Know Where to Go?

"ONLY A CATBIRD IN THE NETS, but I flushed a woodcock, right beside me. First one I've seen that close in years," I remarked, after finishing my first round of the Nature Center's Marsh Trail collecting netted birds for banding.

Woodcocks have always intrigued me with their remarkable long bills, diet of earthworms, and wings that seem to twitter at their abrupt straight line take off. In the spring, I've watched the male in his dramatic zigzag mating display, but those sightings occur in dim twilight when one can rarely see detail. This one I flushed was better lit and so close to me.

These popular game birds may have nested in the Center's open swampy woods area, but will winter in Louisiana, Mississippi, or Alabama.

On the second round of net-emptying, I found a shy, monochromatic, and rather bedraggled gray-cheeked thrush, probably on his way from Canadian nesting grounds to the West Indies or Venezuela. Despite these discoveries, I was discouraged at the meager findings on this foggy morning of August 27th.

One net had two male American goldfinches, already beginning to lose their bright summer dress. They had been rollercoasting our fields and roadsides all summer, stopping to inspect tall sunflower heads in local gardens, hoping for a ripe seed or two.

With the last net I hit the jackpot—a flock of birds at last. First a stunning yellow-throated vireo, he of the yellow spectacles and slightly hooked bill.

Near him in the net was a grayish warbling vireo, easily confused in this season with another summer visitor, the Tennessee warbler. A quick check for a slight hook in the bill settled the vireo identification. The bird had a clear eyebrow stripe, the superciliary, as the ornithologists say.

There were three Tennessee warblers. The bright chartreuse wash on the lower back is a reliable field mark in the fall. This four and one-half inch bird with white undertail coverts is a rare nester in the Upper Peninsula, preferring the boreal forest bogs lying north of the United States.

The charming common yellowthroat had one representative in my jackpot net. The young male's gray eye mask will be solid black by spring giving him his distinctive bandit look. His throat was the characteristic brilliant yellow.

There was also a veery, a member of the thrush family often confused with its cousins. Breaking up forests with roads and homes threatens this and other species that nest in hollows in the ground in quiet places.

One of the Center's staff banders was tending other nets and brought back a radiant magnolia warbler. This species nests in Michigan's Upper Peninsula and across Canada, and winters in Panama. The most helpful field mark in both sexes of magnolias of any age is the broad white stripe across the tail.

My last bird of the morning was an iridescent green female ruby-throated hummingbird. As I removed her from the net ever so carefully, tiny, tiny feathers flew, telling me she was quite new to the world, still molting natal down. Her throat was white, as a first year male's would be, but the corners of her tail were white, assuring me of her sex.

As I was admiring the hummingbird, noting the amazing strength of her heartbeat, she kept talking to me with a queer little squeaky chip of protest. I released her gently. She requires a special banding permit.

I wonder if she's safe from the parasitism of cowbirds. Is her open nest too small to hold their large eggs?

Whenever I'm banding, I marvel anew at the very special gifts our birds have which enable them to fly great distances, to sing, to procreate, and to conduct their migrations with nary a map, compass, or computer printout.

September 9, 1995

Christmas Bird Counts

CHRISTMAS BIRD COUNTS, a nationwide Audubon Society tradition since 1900, occur at a season when many birders are too involved in accustomed family rituals to participate, but those who can break away often have eye-opening experiences.

On December 20th, 1997, we found 48 eastern bluebirds, 8 in my binoculars at once. Who would expect such grace and style in December, a real Christmas gift in itself. Among other species, we located 8 northern flickers, 3 song sparrows, 4 American robins, 3 golden-crowned kinglets, and 5 red-tailed hawks.

At one point, I had a stunning white-throated sparrow framed by three northern cardinals all posing in a snowy bush. No greeting card designer could ask for anything lovelier.

Our day's list of 34 species included: 85 chickadees, 8 titmice, 74 goldfinches, 48 cardinals, 33 mourning doves, 18 house finches, and 28 white-breasted nuthatches.

At woodland edges, a screech owl tape was played

briefly to attract curious birds; there is always a good response, especially from chickadees. Tape-playing must be limited because it would be a severe disservice to make birds indifferent to a predator call through over-familiarity.

Winter guests, in from the north in search of food, included a delightful 133 American tree sparrows, 112 dark-eyed juncos, two red-breasted nuthatches, and thirty-five common redpolls.

A barred owl seen at eye-level was a treat. In fifty years of this Battle Creek count, a total of 131 species has been found.

On December 22d, our team totalled thirty-two species. We went owling in the dark and enjoyed single candles glowing in farm house windows, a restful change from sometimes gaudy holiday lights. Two screech owls responded to a tape. Tree silhouettes were lovely in snowy woods as the sky lightened. One privilege of Christmas counts is to be in unusual places at unusual times.

The day's total of 610 birds included a sharp-shinned hawk, plus hundreds of rock doves and starlings enjoying the heat on grain dryer roofs. One purple finch, two kestrels, three hermit thrushes, and six horned larks were special treats. But no snow buntings.

I learned one good lesson from my knowledgeable driver: really look, don't just guess. In passing a house feeder, I casually called an all-black bird on a feeder a starling. The astute driver continued on several hundred yards and said, "Let's go back. A starling in winter isn't all black. He's speckled and he isn't usually on a feeder. Maybe it's a brown-headed cowbird who should have migrated but didn't." We retraced our route, waited a minute, and presto—it was a brown-headed cowbird, our only one for the day. I was amazed—and ashamed— to be pleased at seeing a cowbird because of its pernicious brood parasite habit. But on this one-time occasion, he rated four stars for jumping on our list.

As part of last year's count, on December 27th, I monitored a set of feeders for three and one-half hours. It was a bright day after three inches of fresh snowfall. At feeders, one reports only the maximum number of birds of each species seen at any one time, not the individual visits. I listed eight common feeder species plus juncos on the ground, a male red-bellied woodpecker, and a lone red-breasted nuthatch. Maybe they were enjoying the delightful orange-rosy sunrise glow visible through the snowy pine planting. A titmouse fed right beside a fox squirrel, apparently not threatened by his size.

On December 29th, on another route, we stopped in the dark to listen for owls. By the time window candles were dimmed, we had made nineteen owling stops and recorded two great-horned, one screech, and one barred owl.

We prowled this area until noon. We were delighted

to find nine stunning evening grosbeaks in a tree and later twenty more near a house feeder where the resident told us she hoped they'd go away "because they're always so hungry." Seventy-five cedar waxwings were resting in one treetop. Pine siskins pecked at buds high in a large oak tree. Golden-crowned kinglets were lingering. Perhaps they like winterberry's scarlet fruit, often rare but plentiful in 1997.

Northern refugees included sixty-one juncos and forty-one tree sparrows. An active tiny winter wren searching low shrubs along an open stream was my Christmas gift of the trip. An estimated total of thirty-three species and 696 individuals was satisfying for a mizzly December day.

In 1979, Adams published a booklet of bar graphs of Kalamazoo area birds. Of twenty-eight land birds he listed as being regular and common in December, we saw all but one, the snow bunting. Of sixteen birds he listed as regular but rare, we saw five.

On New Year's Day, I watched a varied and well-stocked set of feeders with fourteen species of birds coming and going constantly. A mild day for the season, I had titmice, goldfinches, cardinals, downy woodpeckers, mourning doves, nuthatches, chickadees, house finches, and house sparrows. Juncos and tree and white-throated sparrows were especially welcome northern visitors. Black squirrels scurried around, vacuuming up what ground birds missed.

Reviewing a Fairbanks, Alaska, newspaper story of their 1996 Christmas count, one learns that 150 birders went out at twenty-five degrees below zero and found 2,603 birds of twenty-nine species. They even had an American coot and a golden-crowned kinglet.

December 5 and 12, 1998

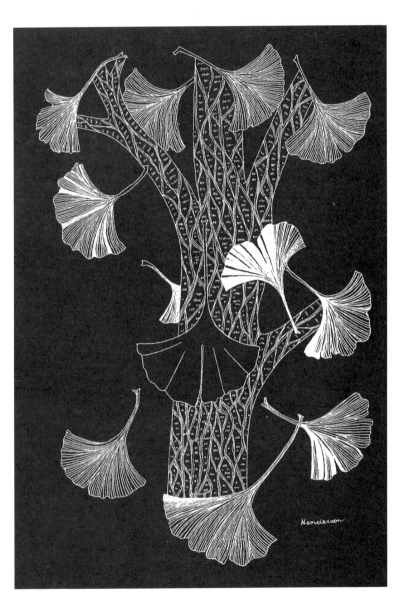

About Trees

Springtime Trees

Friendship is a sheltering tree.
Samuel Coleridge

IN WINTER, EVERGREEN TREES prove their warm friendship to us in the protection given our homes by thousands of planted shelter belts. Their friendship to wildlife is also very important, because they provide food and safe cover from inclement weather and predators. Mammals and birds eat needles from evergreens as well as seeds retrieved from cones. Birds roost in cavities or close to trunks where thick branches shut out the worst of sleet, snow, and cold.

But now, with spring in sight, we are made more aware of the friendly ways of trees. When daylight hours started to increase in January, male catkins on hazelnuts lengthened with amazing speed. By March, sap began to run up maple trunks as unseen buds far above started secret expansion.

Bark on red osier-dogwood shrubs takes on a more intense shade of red when sap runs freely again. If you have them in your plantings, cutting out several branches each spring will stimulate growth of new red material. Prune right at the ground in late winter before leaves emerge. This dogwood is especially desirable because it flowers all summer long, even in late September. White fruits, with high fat content, are a favorite food of birds.

Everyone knows and loves the pussy-willow, a medium-sized shrub whose twigs have a maroon tinge and whose furry gray catkin buds are admired by all. Like its *Salix* relatives, pussy-willows have only one bud scale, whereas other trees have a pair. Sometimes, even in autumn, vagrant bits of silver gray fluff are visible at tips of the scale. Pick off that single scale and there's your little pussy waiting for spring.

In walking mixed woods, one notices red cedars with shredded and stripped bark which red and flying squirrels have removed for nesting. I've never been witness to squirrels doing the stripping, but damage on tree trunks and stuffing of nest boxes are unmistakable proof.

Marcel Marceau, the French master of pantomime, bought a 250-year-old farmhouse with only four trees on the property. Later he wrote; "I have planted more than 2,500 now and have created a forest. To me, trees are symbols of life." Michigan could use increased numbers of people with this attitude as more and more of our open and natural areas become housing, industrial, and parking sites, the all too familiar urban sprawl syndrome.

If you want more trees, and funds are short, try

gathering seeds and growing your own. We have shoulder-high shingle oak trees grown from acorns planted in 1991. Protection from rabbits and squirrels is essential but results are often gratifying.

A recent newspaper story reported that ecologists have found a small patch of Brazilian rain forest containing 476 tree species, more than any spot of similar size ever studied—only two and a half acres. A similar patch in our temperate forest would contain only two to twenty species.

Another problem we have, besides loss of open land, is the weakening of trees by overdoses of ozone and sulfur dioxides in the air. Such poisons eventually will kill the trees. Tip necrosis and blotchy spotting on needles of white pine trees are caused by air pollution. Pines near parking lots often suffer, even die, from over exposure. The Black Forest in Germany has experienced serious losses caused by pollution blown from industrial areas many miles away.

There has been considerable concern in maple syrup-producing areas about the tree's health, but Canadian studies indicate that injury is from drought, disease, and overtapping rather than from pollution. Because sugar maples can live to be 300 years old, premature loss is particularly unfortunate.

If you know the whereabouts of linden, also called basswood, check out the zigzag twigs for unusual waxy, scarlet buds. They were perfect round globes most of the winter, but now are assuming a pointed shape, and the red is fading as spring green takes over. The buds are even pleasant tasting. Try a nibble. Fragrant cream-colored flowers do not appear on this well shaped tree until July. Later still, hard pea-like seeds will form, each with a long personal parachute to help waft it away from the parent tree helping to perpetuate the species. In early American days, the large heart-shaped leaves were dried and stored in the barn for winter cattle food, so plentiful were the trees.

Many oaks and beeches still hold last year's leaves. Oak leaves have stayed thick and crisp, but beech leaves have bleached and thinned to a warm gauzy beige. As spring wears on, cells of abscission finally develop and new buds push off old leaves.

Under red oaks, you may find large sprouting acorns. Their exposed flesh is often dramatically red and long slender roots are already fastened in the ground. Transplant one of these with care, and in a few years you will have one of the noblest trees of the forest for your very own. Oaks in general are slow growing, but red oaks are exceptions to the rule.

Spicebush shrubs in moist woods provide tiny bright yellow flower globes by mid-April. It's easy to walk right by them when in full blossom if you're not watching closely. Petalless flowers appear before the aromatic leaves, cling tightly to the stem, and are arranged with three to six tiny florets in a small cluster. Spicebush develops gleaming, brilliant scarlet berries in October. Watch for them, especially in bottom land areas. Watch, too, for the angular chrysalises of spicebush butterflies that choose spicebush, sassafras, and other members of the laurel family for winter homes, fastening their containers to branches with loops of silk. Nectar from Joe Pye weed, *Impatiens*, and honeysuckles are favorite foods of this butterfly.

April 4, 1998

Dogwoods

FLOWERING DOGWOOD TREES are surely one of southern Michigan's loveliest delights throughout the year. In spring, large white blossoms are spectacular; their spreading upturned branch forms are graceful. The foliage is verdant all summer, turning many different shades from apricot to soft maroon in autumn. Abundant clusters of brilliant scarlet fruits in September attract migrating thrushes, flickers, cardinals, and cedar waxwings.

Eastman, in *The Book of Forest and Thicket*, tells us "the scarlet fruits are high in fat content (twenty-four percent by weight) much worth eating by birds." The bright seeds disappear within days of their ripening so popular are they. He also tells us the seeds "are bitter and unpalatable to humans."

In winter, the distinctive dome-shaped flower buds hold snow crystals. Rabbits are winter nibblers on twigs and bark of young dogwoods.

Flowering dogwoods are frequent not only in the understory of many local hardwood forests but, because they propagate easily by layering or seed, they are also used extensively in landscape planting. They are small, rather slow-growing, usually not attaining over fifteen to twenty feet. The tallest *Cornus florida* in Michigan, in Lenawee County, measures an amazing fifty-two feet.

As trees age, the bark develops an unusual checkered appearance resembling alligator hide. There is often a purplish cast to young twigs.

The large white petals on flowering dogwood are really not petals at all but are what botanists call petaloid bracts. The true, small, four-petalled flowers are bunched in dense clusters in the center of each blossom.

Dogwood leaves have parallel veins which curve to leaf tip rather than straight out to the edge. Like branches, they are always in opposite arrangement on this tree.

An old school botany book of Asa Gray's, dated 1880, says of dogwood, "according to common tradition, flowering just at the proper time for planting Indian Corn." Indians used dogwood bark for obtaining a scarlet dye and also as a substitute for tobacco, calling it kinnikinnick. Boiled, the dark inner bark was used for treatment of fevers.

A pink form of flowering dogwood is popular. When an urban professional building was being constructed, the physician instructed the architect to design the structure around the existing tree. All hail to those who preserve our trees!

Three of the flowering dogwood's shrubby relatives are natives: gray, red osier-, and alternate-leaved. The gray, or panicled, flourish in fence rows and at the edge of swamps. They are often both plentiful and dense because they spread vegetatively as well as by seed. Twigs are gray, and white fruits follow small white flowers. When fruits are ripening, their stems are bright red, later fading to gray. This shrub is popular with birds for nesting because opposite branching arrangements provide firm support.

Red osier-dogwood, a swamp species, has red waxy twigs with inner channels of white pith which take up more than one-third of the stem breadth. The more mature the branch, the grayer it will be—like human hair—so nurserymen remove one-fourth of the plant each year in early spring to keep new bright red twigs coming. Clusters of tiny white flowers resemble gray dogwood's except that the clusters are round-topped rather than conical. Red osier- is unusual because flowers may be found all summer long.

Alternate-leaved dogwood—pagoda dogwood— another native understory species, likes tamarack swamps or rich moist woodland. It is the only dogwood that doesn't fit in the opposite growth mnemonic *MAD-CAP-Horse* group: *M*aple, *A*sh, *D*ogwood, *CAP*ri-foli-aceae (honeysuckles), *Horse*-chestnut. Its leaves are clustered or whorled at the ends of branches, giving a storied effect.

In their 1947 publication, *Flora of Kalamazoo County, Michigan*, Clarence and Florence Hanes spoke of an alternate-leaved dogwood in Section 31, Oshtemo Township, located in 1943, which was seven inches in diameter, three feet from the base, as being very large for that species. I wish we could find that tree now to see what fifty-three years have brought to it.

Of all the hundreds of plants from which to choose in this area, I find it interesting that Florence Hanes selected a flowering dogwood spray for the engraving on the headstone she and Clarence share.

June 22, 1996

The Willows

Ah, willow! Willow! Would that I always
possessed thy good spirits.
                                    Henry David Thoreau

WHEN WINTER DAYS LENGTHEN, coloring matter in willow twigs deepens, intensifies, becoming golden yellow in weeping willow trees and orange in black willows. The bright light of spring sunshine coaxes sap to move upward in trunks and branches, launching a new growth year.

There are some seventy species of willow in North America, many of which grow in Michigan. All members of the *Salix* genus bear pollen-bearing and seed-bearing flowers on separate trees.

I particularly enjoy some of the smaller trees and shrubs. In moist roadside hedges and ditches, buds on pussy-willow bushes cast off single mahogany colored bracts to reveal soft and velvety gray male flowers, the pussies known and beloved by all. Soon bees will be busy, gathering golden pollen to use as bread for their young and also gathering nectar from tiny jug-shaped glands at the base of each and every flower. Later, early arriving hummingbirds enjoy pussy-willow pollen when flowers are not yet available. Picked at the furry stage and placed in a vase without water, male branches will stay attractive for months. Placed in water, stems will send out roots and may later be planted. Female flowers, not as furry, develop into hard green capsules which will expand into silky masses of long-haired seeds.

Two smaller willow shrubs found in undisturbed areas and which have always charmed me, are the prairie willow and the hoary willow. Prairie willows have clustered, yellowish stems only three or four feet high. Attractive furry buds begin to open before the leaves by the end of March. These small shrubs are found in sunny open prairie areas where summer soils are often dry.

Distinctive hoary willows, found in cold bogs in glaciated areas, are so named for the remarkably dense white hairs covering the undersides of small canoe-shaped leaves. Leaf edges are turned under, revolute as botanists say. Hoary willow develops fuzzy catkins too, but the special characteristic is the densely matted hairs.

If you're in a wet area hunting for hoary willow, watch for the bright stems of red osier-dogwood shrubs, whose twig coloring intensifies in early spring just as willow twigs do. Even sassafras twigs become greener.

Large willows develop short stout trunks, the largest of any Michigan tree species. Record black, crack, and white willows have trunks over 300 inches in circumference, measured four feet from the ground. Black willows often trace stream edges for considerable distances. As Isaiah phrased it long ago: "They shall spring among the grasses, as willows by the water courses."

Trunks are often surrounded by suckers creating dense shoulder-high growth. Such suckers, and often brittle twigs, break off easily. When carried downstream, they lodge and take root. Eventually, large root masses develop, helping hold banks in place.

An interesting inhabitant of willows that makes her presence known is a small gnat. She lays eggs in twig tips, inhibiting growth and causing leaves to be dwarfed and overlapped into a furry-edged gray-brown cone. These nests protect the larvae who will emerge in the spring as delicate little flies. The wooly "pine cone" growth stays on the branch permanently.

Close-grained willow wood is tough, soft, and light. Properly seasoned, it has many uses such as wooden shoes and kitchen articles. My spies tell me that willow wood makes wonderful whistles, but that handicraft is a skill I never acquired.

Viceroy butterflies' larvae spend their winter rolled up lengthwise in a willow leaf cradle on a lower branch of a host tree. The gray, humpbacked, caterpillar's head plugs the opening.

It would be nice if I could spirit you all away to Arctic Circle areas to study some of the twenty willow species surviving there. Because of incredibly strong prevailing winter winds, all plants must stay below the snow or perish. Therefore, willows act more like vines than trees, clinging to rock surfaces in protected areas. Growth is lateral, not vertical, as willows become dwarf shrubs. Annual growth rates are extremely slow; it takes 100 years to get a trunk the size of one's thumb.

Arctic willow catkins secrete large amounts of pollen on bright red anthers. Plentiful filament fur, made up of clear transparent hairs, functioning like greenhouse windows, raises temperatures four to five degrees, a clear advantage to plant development. The combination of fur and bright red color creates most appealing flowers—a rare sight in the Arctic.

March 17, 1998

Birds Need Trees

Trees are a part of our everyday life, taken for granted in this climate. But have you ever stopped to think about what they mean to birds, the many ways birds are affected by their presence or absence?

Most of our year-round residents are seed and nut eaters who find food from or on woody plants all winter. Birds dependent on insect, water, or vegetative diets migrate south, away from snow and ice cover. Most of those who stay have structural body adaptations that allow them to eat oak, hickory, beech, and hazelnuts, all hard-shelled crops.

In the mid 1940s, scientists studying breeding bird density in different habitats came up with interesting statistics. The highest figure for United States forests was 762 adult birds per 100 acres of virgin spruce forests in West Virginia. Michigan had 118 adults for 100 acres of aspen-red maple forest and 292 in a cedar-balsam forest.

Woodpeckers are tree-dependent, drilling in old wood for insects and carving holes for roosting and nesting. Their bodies are wonderfully adapted with extra cranial musculature to support these habits, so the force of pounding will not pop their eyes right out of their heads. They peck at holes from different directions, just like a good human woodchopper. Bills are heavy, strong, and often chisel-tipped. The flexible tongues with barbed edges are extensible, permitting insertion for some distance into rotten labyrinths in quest of food.

A sapsucker's main nourishment is the sap obtained by drilling rows and rows of holes in trunks of many different trees and waiting a few minutes until the holes fill with liquid. In sapsucker nesting areas farther north, favorite trees may die from repeated assaults.

Beechnuts and acorns, often found in great numbers in good years, are favorite foods of woodpeckers, jays, and wild turkeys. Acorn woodpeckers of the west are noted for their unique habit of drilling a good-sized hole in a tree and inserting an acorn, thus creating a make-shift pantry. One huge California sycamore reportedly has 20,000 acorns dotting its surface.

Many birds have the word tree or wood incorporated in their names. The wood thrush is well named because he prefers to nest in low tree branches, glean for food on the forest floor, and present his lyric twilight ser-enades from secluded woodland spots.

The wood duck, too, is well named because, rare among ducks, he chooses to nest in a natural tree cav-ity rather than on the ground near relatives. I've always wished I could witness an emergence of just-hatched young. They scramble to the cavity's opening and leap to the ground regardless of the hole's height, then waddle to the nearest water under mother's supervision and encouragement.

Whistling-tree ducks and common and hooded mergansers often lay eggs in tree cavities, but red-breasted mergansers prefer well-concealed ground nests under dense protective branches of evergreens and usually near water. Common goldeneyes use cavities six to sixty feet up in elms, maples, and birches.

Iridescent green tree swallows must be so named because of their habit of nesting in holes in trunks. They do not eat tree fruits or sap; instead, they search through the air, especially above ponds, for their major food supply.

Wood storks, with five-foot wingspreads, construct their homes fifty to eighty feet high with five to twenty-five nests per tree. An important courtship procedure is the ceremonial presentation of a stick to a mate, one which may or may not be added to the nest structure. A fair amount of ritual bowing in the treetops accompanies this presentation.

I do not know why tree sparrows and woodcocks are so named; their use of trees is minimal. But no one ever said that nomenclature of our flora and fauna was logical.

Many avian species depend on trees for nesting

materials regardless of where they place them. For example, a house wren will fill every cranny of a bluebird house with sticks of uniform size. Nests may be in tree cavities, as indicated earlier, or they may be open ones supported by or hanging from branches such as those which many warblers, vireos, and flycatchers construct.

A major tragedy in the reduction of tropical rain forests is that our tree-dependent migrant species may have nowhere to go in winter.

December 16, 1995

The Ancient Ginkgo

KALAMAZOO IS BLESSED with many tall and strong ornamental trees as well as interesting and different ones. One species admired by many is the unique curiosity known as the ginkgo. There are numerous examples; they are planted on two sides of the federal courthouse building. Their reaching branches, seeking the light, seem to embrace the building. This tree is an especially good choice for the site because it is well-known for surviving air pollution. It also is more fungus and insect resistant than many trees and is tolerant of cold weather. In big cities, parkways often are lined with them. The Nature Center's Arboretum has several fine ginkgos. West of the Hummingbird and Butterfly Garden, one was planted in 1972 and another in 1982. The older one, given by Kalamazoo College when the land was still a hay field, has grown luxuriant foliage. Others are in the barnyard area. Another beautiful specimen is located in a city park.

Ginkgo biloba is an ancient Chinese species dating back 150 million years to the Mesozoic era. Oddly, it is not presently found in the wild in China and is therefore termed a living fossil. Specimens were brought to Philadelphia from England in 1784 and the tree now grows throughout most of the United States. Hardy in the southern half of Michigan, the largest specimen is in Hillsdale County with a girth of 134 inches and a height of ninety-four feet.

The tree's fan-shaped leaves are one of its special charms. Gray-green and borne on rather long, flexible stems, they are both velvety and leathery, usually divided at the summit, and heavily ribbed. Leaves stay on the tree until late in autumn, turn a radiant, clear yellow, and tend to drop all at once, apparently in response to sudden temperature change. The mass of golden leaves accumulated under a large tree is truly a delight. I can remember being unable to resist their beauty, placing a few of them on all the desks in our office.

Another unique specialty is the arrangement of fine circular markings on the thickened spur stubs or shoots, a delicate design worth studying under a hand lens.

The word ginkgo routinely is misspelled in written materials of all kind, because *kg* is not a common combination. Perhaps saying "the gink goes" will help you. The name means silver nut in Asian languages, because the tasty kernel inside the plum-like, ill-smelling pulpy fruit is indeed silver. These nuts are considered festive foods in the Orient where trees are widely grown. They are our oldest cultivated nut tree.

Wind-pollinated male flowers, resembling catkins, are borne on trees separate from female trees with their acorn-like flowers. The disagreeable odor of decaying fruit on female trees dictates planting of male specimens. The Gull Lake campus of Michigan State University—the Kellogg Laboratories—has a large female tree, but specimens I've seen are male.

Slow growing, ginkgoes are generally pyramidal in shape with stout trunks and relatively few up-stretching curved branches. They frequently are called maidenhair trees because their elegant leaf shape resembles leaflets of the maidenhair fern. They can live to be over 100 years old.

Their corky, grayish bark is irregularly fissured and becomes deeply furrowed in old age. The finely textured wood is white but too soft and weak to be useful for anything more than making chessmen or art objects.

In China and India, people have used ginkgo leaves in therapeutic ways for at least 3,000 years, for ailments varying from coughs to frostbite. Their magical elixirs guaranteed long life. Pharmaceutical use in the United States is recent and limited to problems with veins.

October 5, 1996

Eastern White Pine

LET ME INTRODUCE MYSELF. I am an eastern white pine tree. I am writing to celebrate my life, to tell you about my many splendors. I live in well-drained sandy areas of northeastern North America, thriving as far northeast as Newfoundland, as far northwest as Lake Winnipeg, and south in the Appalachians to Georgia.

My family is a large one, with about fifty distant relatives scattered over the country. Some scholars even say I have ninety relatives, each one adapted to different soil, water, light, and temperature conditions. When transplanted elsewhere, most of us will grow, but not as luxuriantly as in our home habitat.

As early as 1605, people shipped some of my ancestors as logs to England to be used as ship masts. A century later, young trees were taken to Europe and forests of them grown for their value as timber.

I belong to the pine cone family. My Latin name is *Pinus strobus*; *Pinus* is my genus, and *strobus* is Greek and Latin for cone.

Long a monarch of the eastern forest and designated

as Michigan's state tree, I am known for my great size and height as well as for my graceful tapering shape and delicate flexible plumes terminating each shoot. I have the softest needles of any pine and can be identified easily because I always have five needles per bundle, three to six inches long. Other pines have sheathed clusters of just two or three. A simple way to remember me is that there are five letters in the word white and five needles in a cluster. My triangular needles are bluish-green with a pointed tip and white lines on two of the three sides. After three to five years, the whorls of needles turn brown and drop in autumn, creating thick, springy carpets.

I am the tallest pine east of the Rockies. Only the sugar pine of the Pacific coast tops me. Early Michigan lumbermen reported finding white pines with straight trunks six feet in diameter and crowns reaching to 200 feet, with occasional trees as old as 350 years. Several have shown rings representing at least 450 years of growth. Nowadays, lumbermen cut trees at sixty to eighty feet tall. The Michigan champion white pine, 201 feet tall, with a sixty-three-foot crown spread, is at the Huron Mountain Club, near Marquette.

A sun-lover, I outstrip my neighbors in height, usually growing with hardwoods or hemlock and red pine. Sometimes I'm found growing in pure stands, especially in the north woods, my favorite habitat. The Estivant Pines Nature Sanctuary, south of Copper Harbor, is a classic forest of virgin white pines, a living museum site to explore, to listen to tree voices murmuring.

In my early weeks of growth I have a tap root, making me easy to transplant, but when I'm older, I develop more lateral roots. Winter storms may uproot me. Wind-thrown trunks are common farther north on shallow, rocky soils. My bark is thick, smooth, and greenish-brown at first, but in old age, the exposed part is deeply fissured and may be as much as four inches thick with broad, flat-topped, dark gray longitudinal ridges. The surface is often streaked with white resin drippings.

Annual growth in a good year can be phenomenal, as much as four feet in height and an inch in trunk diameter. Such adolescent spurts often give me an odd appearance, but the long bare trunk sections admit light, keeping needles and inner bark green. Eastman, in *The Book of Forest and Thicket*, writes of the distinctive "feathery, stacked appearance" of white pines.

Close inspection of my branches in winter will disclose a terminal cluster of tiny buds, much relished by foraging hungry squirrels and deer. Their removal permanently alters the tree's natural symmetry because, undisturbed, those buds surrounding the end would become branches, whorled around a larger branch.

Approximation of my age can be determined by starting at the top and counting the number of whorls of three to six horizontal branches you encounter as you move down. Unfortuntely, near the bottom some of the oldest branches will have dropped and bark will have healed over the scars.

In old age, struggle with wind storms and lightning damage will have broken many branches, giving me a rugged, picturesque look as I approach your Social Security age. White pines scattered along exposed ridges and shores of islands dotting the northern Great Lakes show up in a super canopy all their own, crippled veterans protruding far above surrounding vegetation, providing lookouts for hawks, eagles, and owls.

In May, if I'm at least fifteen years old, I produce attractive, closely-packed, pollen-bearing male cones or flowers which resemble red raspberries. When the sacs split, amazingly abundant supplies of gold dust float away, settling in streaky masses on streets and cars. These staminate cones are scattered well over the tree in order to provide the prodigious amounts of pollen grains which wind pollination requires. Fading cones fall to the ground. Female flowers, found only in upper branches and almost hidden there, are bright pink with purple margins. If they receive male pollen bodies at the right time, they will, by August of the second year, become five to eight inches long, curved, thornless, woody cones, bearing mature seeds under long scales. Bumper crops occur irregularly, causing wildlife hardship in off years.

One problem with white pines in cities is that air

pollution causes tip necrosis, death of needle tips. Eastman has written at length of blister rust disease and insect plagues common to white pines, but he also tells us that chopped spring needles make fine tea, containing as much vitamin C as an equal weight of lemons. Pine pitch, sticky, sticky exudate, has historic use for waterproofing and even glue. Sap is still used for making turpentine.

You will find me grown in extensive plantations, in order to meet the endless demand for my excellent wood—soft, durable, light, and straight grained—which has a wider range of uses than any other tree species. I'm not good for firewood because burning pitch makes many sparks.

From a conservation standpoint, always a concern these days, I am a valuable member of natural habitats, near the top in importance to wildlife. I provide shelter to many species and nest sites for local jays, crows, and mourning doves. In the north, ravens, grosbeaks, and half a dozen warbler species nest in my branches. Masses of old needles on the ground support mushroom species, providing small mammals food. Many bird species eat my seeds. Crossbills are specially adapted to wrest the seed from deep-in-cone crevices; they obtain as much as fifty percent of their total food intake from pine seeds. These birds are rare in certain parts of the country, but there is a record of a white-winged female eating sunflower and thistle seed on a bitter winter day in northern Indiana. Grouse eat my needles and eastern bluebirds will build their entire nest with them. Growing readily from seed and having attractive year-round foliage, I am proud that my trees are widely used in shelter belts, ornamental plantings, and as background vegetation. An attractive spring display is that of white pines amid a large array of golden daffodils, a lovely color contrast.

January 25, 1997

Autumn in the Woods

HAS THAT TREE, whose autumn color changes you especially enjoy, showed its brilliant tips? I used to keep watch on a seventy-five-foot black gum which by August 15th flaunted—somewhere in its branches—a scarlet leaf lobe or two, my first hint of fall.

Each woods walker has personal reasons for enjoying the arrival of autumn. It may be the crunching of leaves under foot, daily changes in the color palette, sudden crispness of the weather, or arrival of the season's migrant birds. For some, it means that new evidence surfaces to help in identifying unknown trees. It may be that seeds appearing on trees, seemingly suddenly, can reveal the species.

Truly, one can't mistake the distinctive product of a spiny osage orange tree for anything else, because of its large, grainy, lime-green, globular shapes. Larger than a tennis ball, and sometimes called hedge apple, this fruit contains a sticky latex milk and is heavily scented. I shall never forget the year a crafts person suggested that the fruit slices, if well dried, were attractive in winter arrangements. Instructions were to cut the fruit—a nasty, sticky job—and then dry them in a slow oven for an hour. Don't do it. It took a week to get the awful smell out of my house. Perhaps the segments are attractive, but there must be a better way.

Widely used in the early Midwest for hedging and fencing, osage oranges are no longer common because mature trees took too much space from the farm. With their passing, many a bird lost a comfortable, safe nest site. In the Kalamazoo area, one occasionally finds roadsides littered with these sticky green balls, but barbed wire and the no-fence-at-all-fad have relegated hedge apples to the antiques list.

At the Nature Center, follow the path through the Arboretum that leads to the barn, keeping watch on the right for the Kentucky coffee tree and its heavy, thick, mahogany-colored pods. At six to ten inches in length, they are among the largest pods in America. Hanging through the winter, the six or more hard round seeds rattle in the big pods as the sweetish but inedible sticky pulp dries up. Members of the pea family, the trees have large leaves, doubly compound, resembling those of honey and bristly locust. They turn a delightful, reflective lemon yellow. The seeds were used, rather unsatisfactorily, as a substitute for coffee beans in backwoods country where tropical beans were expensive and hard to come by.

A third tree, whose unusual fruit is a diagnostic

characteristic when autumn is on the horizon, is the hop hornbeam, a small species with ax-handle-hard wood like that of osage orange. A birch family member, its rather elm-like, finely toothed leaves are thin, but tough, lacking in outward distinction. The flat seeds—one-third of an inch long— come packed in small, inflated, papery, green packages and are gathered into hop-like clusters, hence the name. It's easy to grow new trees from these seeds—if you can wait for two years until they germinate. Leaves turn a clear yellow in the fall, making a delightful understory, especially when combined with the tall red maples whose company it favors.

A tree that can always be identified by the lemony odor of its leaves, if perchance any are low enough to be reached, is the black walnut. Large, light green, pulpy hulled fruits occur annually in great numbers. One local resident, who needed to mow his lawn during fruit fall, persuaded his five-year-old twins to collect large piles of nuts at the foot of his driveway. I estimated 100 nuts in one pile and at least 200 in each of the other two. What a find for the native red and fox squirrels! Too bad that saving each single nut entails a full round trip to and from the hiding spot.

I remember another autumn when a friend tediously collected two five-gallon pails of walnuts from our lawn to save our ankles from certain fracture. He put the full pails under the barn eaves. Next morning, to our surprise, both were completely empty. The woodsheds nearby looked as if the squirrels had decorated them for Christmas, with round green ornaments tucked into every crack and opening in the stacked firewood.

September 25, 1999

Seeds

IF SOMEONE GAVE YOU a hard green ball, smaller than a tennis ball but larger than a golf ball that was a little sticky and had a lemony fragrance, could you identify it? Or if you had a cluster of marble-sized balls buried in green ruffles? Or a three-inch long woody item composed of narrow wings, each one bumpy at the bottom? Or a walnut-sized, green ovate shape with inconspicuous ribs and fibers at each end? Or a tiny, tiny, flattish acorn with a shallow flat cap? Or a very large acorn also with a shallow flat cap?

In *Pocket Guide to the Trees*, Rutherford Platt said: "Take any tree. Hang a sign on it announcing 'Something marvelous is going on here.'" One of the marvelous things going on this time of year is the maturation of tree seeds. Every species has a different and distinct way of presenting its fruits. They come in many sizes and shapes with secret methods to increase chances of successful reproduction. An immense portion of a tree's energy goes into manufacturing large amounts of cellulose tissue to protect developing seeds from raiding insects as well as from animals, including birds, that would eat them before maturity.

Evergreen family members have developed elaborate protective systems. In good seed years, the bottom petals of cones harbor sheer membranes tipped with tiny hard seeds. And because that minute seed holds the future of the race within it, the woody cone is designed to open its petals in good weather and close them tightly when it's wet. Cones on the ground, long empty and perhaps several years old, still open and close with the rains. What a magical mechanism.

Jeffrey pine cones are huge, frequently fifteen inches long, prickly and purplish at maturity and smelling of pineapples. Bristlecone pines have fragile sharp, curved, resiny prickles on their fruit. One wonders why the protective device, because cones open annually, scattering generous crops of seed each year in late September. Someone who likes to eat them must come hunting too early before seed is mature, hence the sharp prickle.

Michigan's state tree, the eastern white pine, does not mature for fifteen to twenty years and then takes two seasons to produce fertile cones. By September, the long sticky cones open to discharge delicate gossamer wings attached to pinhead-sized seeds. The wings may carry them as much as 1,000 yards.

In sandy areas, our jack pines bear cones in pairs when the tree is four to eight years old. Cones are narrow, hard, and always curved and cling tightly to the branch. Taking two years to mature, they may not open for another twenty-five. It often takes fire to crack the cone, enabling it to discharge its seeds.

Tamaracks, fond of swampy ground, bear half-inch long cones that are a delightful rose color when they emerge in June. By fall, they are brown and the scales spread to free the winged seed.

Woody petals of spruce cones are softer than those of pines, a helpful distinction. In spring, these stand up straight, but after fertilization, mature cones—with evenly spaced, rhythmically arranged petals—hang down and release seeds the first season.

I'm especially fond of the small and unusually plentiful cones of hemlocks, a northern species at the edge of its range here. Soft half-inch cones appear when the trees are twenty years old. Two light brown seeds grow under each fertile scale, seeds so small it takes 400,000 to make a pound. Winter resident birds forage happily on them.

Hardy catalpas have easy to recognize heart-shaped leaves and long, narrow, bean-like fruits with many seeds. These unique and often plentiful pods stay on trees all winter and release flat, winged seeds in spring.

Honey locusts are as famous for their vicious, long-forked spines on trunks and lower branches as for their foot-long flat but twisted pods. A member of the legume family, their seeds contain a nutritious, sweet, succulent pulp at early stages and are much sought after by small rodents. Most horticultural varieties of locusts have the unique pods, but lack thorns. Trees bear fertile seeds early, but have large crops only every three to five years.

Another interesting tree seed is that of our stately beech, again one with built-in prickly devices to protect fruits until full maturity. Small barbed burs drop and open in September, often in great numbers. Two or three leathery triangular sweet-meated nuts are welcomed by blue jays, tufted titmice, and wild turkeys. Beech mast was a staple food of the passenger pigeons. Like locust trees, large crops of seeds often do not occur every year.

Prickliest of all tree seeds to be found locally are those of the sweet gum. Its unique, woody, horn-tipped ball releases seeds in the fall but the container overwinters on the tree. A composite, round bur, it has woody, closely-connected capsules containing the seeds. At maturity, the capsules open little mouths, making them resemble salt cellars.

Flowering dogwoods, unlike other species mentioned, do not have protective spines or woody coverings; they have clusters of pulpy, egg-shaped fruits. In *The Book of Forest and Thicket*, Eastman said:

> The scarlet fruits are high in fat content (twenty-four percent by weight), much worth eating by birds. Such high energy foods combined with brilliant leaf color represent an evolved relationship called *foliar fruit flagging*; the red color attracts birds (many of them autumn

migrants) which consume the fruits and disperse the seeds in their droppings, often many miles from the original tree.

In case you wondered, the tree seeds described in the first paragraph are those of black walnut, hazelnut, tulip, pignut hickory, pin oak, and red oak.

October 18, 1997

Winter Identification

IDENTIFYING TREES IN WINTER is like doing a large jig-saw puzzle: one assembles available clues to see if a clear image emerges. Sometimes a decision is quick and easy, foolproof, as in noting blackened "potato chip bark" and knowing that makes it definitely a black cherry, noth-ing else. But sometimes, especially with young trees, it's difficult to reach a firm conclusion.

A little practice will help identify some large trees from a distance. Most of us know the familiar vase form of American elms, still to be found in wetland edges. Sugar maples, our sweetest trees, have an oval silhou-ette and many many small branches. Bur oaks are "burly", with low, spreading, knotted, sturdy-looking branches. Watch for them when you're cruising Inter-state 94, because they like sunny, open habitats. Red oaks are woodland types, so their branches ascend in irregular pattern. Try sketching some typical shapes to help fix details in your mind.

One writer says to observe the three Bs: branches, bark, and buds. You can start by checking the pattern of branches and twigs. When branches are clearly op-posite, then choices are strictly limited to a specific group: *MAD-CAP-Horse*. Likewise, if branching pattern is alternate, then your tree is not of that group and your choices are therefore legion.

Bark is another characteristic yielding several firm, easy answers. Beech has satin-smooth, grayish-purple bark, even in old age. Some folks think you should study it holding your head upside down, to visualize shadings more easily. Try that and see what you think. Around the base of the beech, the bark darkens and the woody growth looks like elephant feet.

Ash tree bark has diamond-shaped ridges in the sur-face. Stare at it a minute until the diamonds come clear to you. Hackberries, close cousins of American elms, have thick, sometimes scaly, elongated warty knobs—most distinctive. The dry, dark purple, pea-sized dan-gling berries may linger into winter. Any remaining leaves resemble elm leaves but are thinner, less substan-tial.

Red osier-dogwood shrubs in wetland areas have dark red bark, reddest in March. Sassafras twigs are lus-trous green throughout the year, but especially in late winter. Scratch one slightly to test for its aromatic fra-grance.

Ruddy brown bark on sycamores peels off in thin brittle layers, exposing patches of lighter colored inner bark. White and gray birches wear their familiar white

coats, often chalky or peeling, and are marked by conspicuous dark horizontal lines, called lenticels, openings
that allow gases to exchange. Lenticels are also obvious
on young black cherry trees that have not yet developed
the black flakes typical of maturity. On birches, watch
for winged black scars below each branch. Near the
ground, birch bark is almost black. Yellow birch is a
more northern species, but if you scratch young bark,
you'll find a nice wintergreen fragrance.

Black walnut bark is nearly black, often deeply ridged
and furrowed. A few heavy branches are charactistic.
Diamond shapes can be visualized, although not as
clearly as with ash trees.

Young sugar maples have smooth gray bark, resembling that of beech, but older trees are darker, plated,
or ridged. White oak's light gray scaly bark is sometimes
marked with lighter gray circles, like archery targets,
visible near the base. Not all white oaks have these
marks, but if a circle or two is present, it is definitely a
Quercus alba.

Buds may be helpful in identification. A magnifying glass will help in closeup study. Red maple flower
buds, appropriately red, are clustered at branch tips. A
red maple swamp in late winter presents a panorama of
soft hazy red against blue skies, as the legion clusters of
red and orange flower parts start to explode. Blossoms
open before the leaves, enabling red coloring to domi-
nate and helping pollen to spread freely, unhindered by

leaf presence.

Oaks cluster four, five, or six buds—which may be slightly downy—at twig's end. Leaves are tightly wadded inside. Open one to see them. Hickory family buds are dome shaped and downy, usually bearing only two loose bud scales.

In November, winter buds on basswood—linden—are tiny bright scarlet globes. As days lengthen, the alternately arranged buds stretch out and become more pointed and slightly lopsided. Stout, coarse horse-chestnut twigs have fat, amazingly sticky terminal buds and smaller sticky lateral ones. The shiny gum provides winter protection.

Beech buds are thin, shiny, tightly furled cigars with a reflective, coppery-gold surface, lovely to see in late winter woods. You may have to hunt among still-clinging leaves, but the beauty of the buds makes the effort worthwhile. On tulip trees, glaucous, dark reddish terminal buds are shaped like duck bills.

In August, while the fruit of the year is turning scarlet, flowering dogwood's distinctive winter flower buds emerge. They are flattened domes, like onion-shaped tops of Russian church steeples. In severe winters, when food is hard to find, squirrels and birds may eat all the flower buds leaving only erect stems and greenish, sharp-tipped leaf buds.

Sometimes, when you're trying to identify a tree, there may be leaves on the ground that are helpful. It will depend on how many trees are around and how deep the snow has been, compressing leaves together. Those still hanging usually indicate oak and beech species. In the Fagaceae family, abscission cells, a special separation layer, do not mature in the fall as they do with other trees, but wait until spring bud growth forces old leaves off.

Catkins, or aments as botanists call them, can be helpful when searching for diagnostic clues. Technically, a catkin is a dry, usually elongate—often drooping—scaly spike bearing either male or female flowers. All members of the willow family—trees of the *Populus* and *Salix* genera—are catkin bearers, the latter genus giving us our childhood favorite, the pussy-willow. As pollen on the male flower develops, the tip of each tiny hair will turn golden. The female flower hairs turn green and thicken as the internal seeds develop following fertilization.

Populus members found in the Midwest are the trembling and large-toothed aspens and cottonwood trees. Two nonnatives are lombardy and silver poplars, both widely used in plantings. Catkins can be fat and downy, or long and caterpillary, like cottonwoods.

In wet areas, you may find speckled alders with small persistent cones and catkins that lengthen dramatically as spring advances. The cones, products of female flowers from last year, are not true cones with naked seeds, but have a superficial resemblance.

Hazelnut shrubs, in sunny fence rows and thickets, have stiff male catkins all winter. In March they lengthen, droop, and turn red-gold. According to Eastman, in *The Book of Forest and Thicket*, each catkin has four million pollen grains. Watch carefully in late March for spring's most secretive lady, the tiny female hazelnut flower. She will have no petals, just a starry cluster of minute dark red points that I find especially charming. They will develop into hard-shelled nuts, well buried in ruffled enclosing bracts.

Fruits of several trees that linger on through winter are helpful clues. Acorns, of course, limit choices to oak species. Their size and shape may help you determine which of the many oaks you have found. Depth of the cap is an important detail to study.

Sycamores have golf ball-size dense brown balls on strong, wiry stems, balls which disintegrate into fuzzy masses of hundreds of parachuted seeds clinging to a hard central core. These balls wave in sycamore tops through winter's wildest gales.

Birches may have inch-long dangling pistillate strings of seeds if the finches haven't eaten them all. On a snowy forest floor, watch for charmingly shaped tiny trefoils, the flower scales, and darker centered bits of tissue which are the seeds. Redpolls, goldfinches, and pine siskins spread these far and wide.

Box elder's many drooping canoe paddle clusters are distinctive even at a distance, partly because there are so many on a tree. They tend to cling all winter. Don't forget that box elders are maple family members with leaves and branches in opposite arrangement.

This is a good season to sharpen your identification skills. For example, a black locust has inch-long paired thorns on its twigs and many flat pods which develop from fragrant, showy white blossoms. Eastman also observed that the seeds have impermeable coats, making germination difficult. There are four to eight small flattish ones in three- to four-inch pods, which hang on trees during dormancy. Although black locust is not a Michigan native, it is hardy and widely planted on dunes and banks for erosion control and for decorative purposes. Because it spreads so freely by underground roots, it may become a nuisance, crowding out native species and reducing diversity.

If you look toward the top of a tall tulip tree's straight, unbranched trunk, distinctive erect cone-like clusters are visible on high branches all winter. Even if some seed-bearing parts fall, an outer structure stays. Collections of cone parts—called strobiles or seed cases—around the base of the tree indicate squirrel feeding. Purple finches and cardinals also eat the seeds.

Beeches and horse-chestnuts have distinctive fruits. Despite prickly or hard outer coverings, their popularity with squirrels causes almost total disappearance of the nuts.

Clusters and pancakes of seeds on mountain ash are

dull orange and clearly visible until birds have eaten them.

Many varieties of hawthorns sport spines or thorns which may be slender, straight, sharp, and permanent. American crab trees, with short thick spurs that resemble spines, often hold their little apples until they rot in the spring.

The last useful set of characteristics for identifying winter trees, and a hard one to learn for most people, is the appearance and arrangement of marks on twigs. Understanding the terminology for bud and leaf scars is basic to this skill. Each species has its own official seal of identification, personal characters small enough to require a magnifying glass and lots of patience. As new growth in the spring occurs, scales that protected buds fall off leaving a small scar. When leaves fall, they also leave scars of individual size and shape. Within the scar are tiny dots called bundle traces, which are the ends of veins that carried food and water between leaf and twig. Bundle traces in black walnuts form a U shape, in catalpa a perfect oval, in ash a smiling line. Shagbark hickory scars are heart-shaped with many bundle scars. Learning to observe these distinguishing marks and their differences will improve your twig and tree detective skills.

December 11, 1999, January 1, 15, 29, 2000

Sumacs

SHOULD WE SAY *soomac* as the dictionary suggests, or *shumak* as we often hear it pronounced? Whichever way, it's still a bugaboo tree for me at the moment. I've spent numerous hours trying to reduce the dramatic invasion of staghorn sumac in our old cornfield-cum-woods. Yes, I love the fuzzy fruit pyramids on the picturesque zig-zag branches of the twenty-five-foot trees. They're decorative in snow-filled fields and the small, pleasantly acid drupes are such a boon to spring migrant birds that arrive before new food crops have matured.

Despite its weediness, staghorn sumac is special to me because of a happy memory. I had been a serious bird watcher for more than ten years but had never caught up with one of those stunning gold-and-black evening grosbeaks. They seemed like phantoms to me. But finally, on May 3d on my Indiana country lane, there were an unbelievable fourteen of them stripping the hairy red dried-up fruits from this bush.

But beauty and utility aside, in our woods where we're struggling to encourage native hardwoods and spring flowering trees, the rapid growth and clonal habits of sumac, a common successional shrub, are remarkably detrimental to our efforts.

Rhus typhina is a member of the tropical Cashew family, the Anacardiaceae. The distinctive characteristic that gives the name of staghorn or velvet sumac is the dense pubescence, the fine straight soft hairs covering branchlets and leaf stems. Other native sumacs, fragrant, shining, and smooth species, lack furry coatings.

The staghorn name also fits well because its upper branches spread widely like a stag's horns, a trait especially pleasing in bare winter landscapes.

Alternate, pinnately compound leaves are borne on new wood, therefore at the ends of branches. Stemless leaflets, lance-shaped, sharp-pointed, and serrate, vary in number from eleven to thirty-one, always an odd number. Leaves are much lighter on the undersides and are often hairy along the veins.

Crimson or wine colored bobs, a homely New England name for sumac fruits, ripening in autumn are cone shaped with rough, bunchy surfaces. They may be up to a foot long. The round individual drupes are densely covered with long red hairs. The seed inside the thin flesh coating is light brown and smooth.

Staghorn sumac is in flower in mid-June in southwest Michigan. By mid-July, dense clusters of yellow male flowers—blessed with abundant pollen—have, with the help of small bees and certain flies, done their thing with female flowers. Dense pyramidal cones turn red, flaunting their color above fernlike, almost tropical, leaves.

Nelson Coon's quaint 1957 work, *Using Wayside Plants*, says:

> ...the berries because of their malic—like apples—acid content, are the source of a pleasant and pretty drink. The Indians gave the early Americans the knowledge of this drink, prepared by bruising the fruit in water, straining through a cloth to remove the fine hairs, and adding sugar to taste.

Always heard about it, never tried it.

Staghorn sumac juice is milky and resinous. Inspecting a twig in cross section will show you the central pith. The light, tough wood is an unusual yellow color and can be made into attractive rustic furniture.

The Haneses wrote that staghorn sumac is "common in woods and thickets. Sugarloaf Lake region. A tree with trunk diameter of twelve inches was seen on an embankment south of this lake." I've not seen one that large, but smaller ones are common in sandy or rocky soil in fields, clearings, and thickets. Colonies may number forty or fifty trees, with anemic six-inch babies seeking the light around outside edges. Tending to crowd each other out, dead trees are scattered throughout large roadside stands.

The largest *Rhus typhina* in the southern part of the state is in Cassopolis.

As a boy, Arthur Quick, who lived at Palisades Park on Lake Michigan, learned that sumac leaves contain tannin used in tanning leather. In *Wild Flowers of the Northern States and Canada*, he observed:

> . . . some of the first 'spending money' we boys earned was by picking great numbers of bagfuls of sumac leaves that we carted to the barns and spread out on the floor to dry. Forking them over a few times they were soon cured and after we had secured a sufficient quantity we loaded a hayrack full of these bags of closely-tramped leaves and proudly drove off one Saturday morning to a distant leather tannery. There wasn't much money in it, only a few dollars for the entire load, but after you've earned it yourself, and it's yours, there's a lot of satisfaction in the jingle, isn't there?

The true glory of staghorn sumac comes in early autumn, along with crickets' songs and swarming monarchs, when leaflets develop enough red, crimson, and scarlet shades to challenge any artist. Landscapes are ablaze with the brilliant foliage and the velvety cones last all winter.

Staghorn sumac is the best-known member of the *Rhus* genus, but the less common species, shining, smooth, and fragrant sumacs, are both attractive and interesting. Poison sumac and poison ivy were formerly *Rhus* members, but botanists have given them their own genus, *Toxicodendron*, with a nominal bow to their toxic proclivities.

Fragrant sumac—the least common family member in Michigan—is usually less than three feet tall in the wild, but cultivated in our yards, it may stretch to six or eight feet. I learned *Rhus aromatica* first in northern Indiana where it is a characteristic shrub of the foredunes facing Lake Michigan, associating with jack pine, wafer-leaved hoptree, choke cherry, common milkweed, bittersweet vines, and little bluestem grasses.

In Michigan, Edward Voss shows it scattered over the state, listing it for sixteen counties in "sandy, gravelly soil, open or with oak, hickory and/or pine; river banks; thin soil over limestone (Drummond Island)." In our yards, it seems to thrive in almost any kind of dry soil.

Before leaves open in March or April, fragrant sumac flowers appear with small greenish-yellow blossoms. The foliage is somewhat aromatic if bruised, hence the common name.

Branchlets are smooth or slightly hairy, bearing trifoliate leaflets one to three inches long and coarsely serrate. The clusters of three leaves will remind you of its cousin, poison ivy, but these leaflets are smaller and the terminal one is almost stalkless. If the ovate leaflets should seem just too different from staghorn sumac's long lance-shaped ones, you will immediately recognize the densely hairy red fruits. Instead of being borne in pyramidal cones, they occur in irregular tight clusters on short shoots along the stems, but the overall furry red characteristics are apparent. Small seeds are smooth and slightly flattened.

Fragrant sumac is a desirable shrub for the yard, and propagates easily by layering. It is the only sumac with winter catkins.

Shining or dwarf sumac likes the dry sandy hillsides, lake shores, and black oak woodlands of twenty-one western Michigan counties. This shrub was known to and named by Linnaeus in Sweden, although who took it to him I don't know. Compound leaves on densely pubescent branchlets have seven to fifteen ovate-lanceolate smooth-edged leaflets whose stems are notably winged, a real help in field identification. Leaf surfaces are dark glossy green, smooth and shiny.

Greenish-yellow flowers, in terminal panicles, appear in July and August, with fruit maturing in September and October. Again the fruits, in short-stemmed cones, bear a family resemblance with their red coloring and dense hairiness. The fruit also bears short-stemmed glands. Seeds, smooth and light brown, were used by Indians as a dye. By late summer the foliage charms us with its brilliant reds.

Smooth sumac is an upright shrub common in fence rows, along roadsides, and in untended fields. It is different from close relatives because stems, leaves, and new wood are smooth—or nearly so—and leaf stems are not winged. Leaflets are similar in size and shape to staghorn sumac's.

In June, flowers are in large inflorescences that become red panicles, longer and somewhat more open than those of *Rhus typhina*, with which species it frequently hybridizes. It often spreads out into large vegetative colonies, shutting out other plants. Neighbors are usually box elder, pussytoes, bindweed, black cherry, common cinquefoil, black raspberry, and riverbank grape.

Smooth sumac is probably the most brilliant scarlet of all the sumacs in the fall, with poison sumac in the swamps and bogs a possible exception. Take your choice.

November 4 and 11, 2000

The Holly Family

OUR HOLIDAY SEASON BRINGS with it widespread use of evergreen plants for home decoration. Bringing in greens is a long established custom. Historians say early Teutons hung them inside as a refuge for sylvan spirits suffering from winter's rigors.

One popular green is the foliage of American holly cut from trees grown in the understory of moist southeastern forests. There, holly trees can have a three-foot diameter trunk measurement. Shiny, bright dark green leaves and clusters of scarlet berries are so attractive that they overshadow the stiff sharp spines on tips of wavy-edged leaves. Inconspicuous white flowers appear in mid-spring, with those of the two sexes borne on separate trees. Songbirds, especially thrush family species, are fond of the red fruit and enjoy the shelter which evergreen leaves provide.

One member of the holly family, a shrub variously called Michigan holly, winterberry, or black alder, grows in swampy, lightly wooded areas. The Haneses found winterberry growing throughout Kalamazoo County swamps, particularly at Goose and Sugarloaf lakes.

A friend has an attractive row of these holly bushes right by the front door. Well pruned to the site, they were loaded with red berries in September. As an attractive and hardy native plant, easily cultivated, it should be planted more widely. It can be propagated from seed or softwood cuttings.

Scientists studying Apostle Island vegetation in Lake Superior recorded winterberry as "occasional, bog margins and alder thickets."

Like its southern cousin called yaupon, the winterberry's small yellowish-white flowers are borne on same sex trees, necessitating the presence of at least one tree of each gender if you wish to have a red berry crop. Clusters of eight to fourteen flowers, opening from mid-June into July, appear close to the stem with the female ones smaller and fewer than the male. Winterberry is insect-pollinated by bees. Leaves, three to four inches long, are not evergreen like southern holly, and are not sprinkled with spiny tips. They are oval and serrate-edged and taper to long points. Often, there are a dozen six- to eight-foot vertical trunks in a clump. Bark is gray to reddish brown with warty lenticels, breathing spots for gas exchange. Bright red berries, crowded close to twigs, will stay on the branches until mid-winter, barring bird feasting.

The black alder name is given to winterberry because its leaves turn black before dropping. Protected in the wild in Michigan by the Christmas tree law, the shrub is grown commercially in nurseries for decorative use. Loss of wetlands has seriously reduced its wild populations.

To quote Eastman, from *The Book of Swamp and Bog*: "Winterberry plant associates include black ash, red maple, high-bush blueberry, common elderberry, and poison sumac," all plants which prefer wet feet to dry.

Winterberry fruits, unlike those of dogwood, have a low fat content and are not special favorites of over-wintering birds who wait to eat them until nothing better remains. The hard nutlets contained in the berry are not affected by going through the bird's digestive system and thus contribute to the plant's dispersal. Deer are fond of the berries; if you want to save yours for holiday use, keep them covered with bird netting. Once cut, the branches should be kept in water to prevent shriveling.

In some localities, winterberry is called fever bush because the berries were used, in the days of the colonists, to reduce intermittent fevers, also for treating gangrene and ulcers. Modern books say the berries cause violent vomiting, but the birds seem not to suffer.

Another holly family member found in Michigan tamarack and cedar bogs, and other hard-to-get-to wet places, is the deciduous mountain holly. It is less common than winterberry and typically has only a few crimson berries. It is of no economic importance and rarely used in yard plantings. Mountain holly leaves are small, found on short, spur twigs, smooth-edged, and have a long bristle, a mucro, at the tip. Stem leaves are purple, without hairs.

The Haneses listed mountain holly as infrequent, finding it near "Goose, Sugarloaf, and West lakes; Section 18, Cooper Township; Section 31, Prairie Ronde Township; Section 20, Texas Township."

Although I tramp wet areas every opportunity that comes my way, I have never identified this species. Flower and fruit are so scarce and inconspicuous, that even if they were present, they could be lost to view in the dense shrub-carr—a wetland thicket dominated by tall shrub vegetation—which mountain holly prefers.

December 28, 1996

A Woods Grows Up

Picture the scene of our dream. We envisioned planting many trees, making a sheltering home for native species whose very existence in southwest Michigan is threatened by increasing urban sprawl.

This scenario was located in abandoned cornfields behind the retirement complex where I live. Birch and black cherry already grew there generously, courtesy of various animals. Nature happened, and we just helped it along.

Over the decade, we've planted hundreds of trees and shrubs, ferns, and wildflowers. Shaded and sunny paths, with benches here and there, offer opportunity for quiet solitude as well as vigorous walking. It's nice to have no hand of man visible, restful somehow.

My favorite niche in the woods is a shady one where we nurture pawpaw and elderberry, where a volunteer sassafras colony thrives under a mantle of gray birch, an ancient apple tree, and young trembling aspen. White trillium, bloodroot, violet, toothwort, Virginia bluebell, and several dozen ferns do well there. Hepatica doesn't like the heavy clay, apparently, and just dies out.

One resident brought a northern holly fern with her from Vermont more than twenty years ago. It's been relocated several times, but has settled happily in the woods midst maidenhair, Christmas ferns, and jack-in-the-pulpits. Does one separate such a large fern clump or just let it grow thicker and thicker?

Groups of white pine are placed throughout the woods, offering birds shelter in inclement weather.

In early spring, clusters of snowdrops and drifts of hundreds and hundreds of daffodils make the woodland "a thing of beauty and a joy forever."

A group of small Douglas firs testifies to gardening skills of the resident who germinated the seeds in milk cartons on her window sill. This is the same resident whose family, honoring her ninetieth birthday, gave the woods ninety Chinquapin oak saplings. Hardy volunteers tucked them in on a bitter snowy day, sheltering them in sturdy plastic tubes which detracted from their appearance, but protected them from our ravenous rabbit population.

Colonies of pin, white, red and black oaks, sugar and red maples, redbud, and tulips—all native trees of southwest Michigan and, therefore, comfortably at home here—have been contributed by interested residents.

Plantings of hawthorn, shadbush, hickory, white pine, white cedar, and red osier-dogwood are also here. Flowering dogwoods have struggled against sub-zero temperatures and debilitating disease, but a few are surviving to flower.

Forsythia bushes, too, have suffered from a series of late freezes, but finally flowered well this year; and, because of prolonged mild weather, they glowed with gold for weeks.

In addition to planting incredible numbers of black cherry trees, birds have contributed many, many crabapple trees of various species, a boon for them.

Thirty native prairie crabs, bought from a nursery, survived serious rabbit depredation in a winter of deep snow and are now flowering-size, adding beauty and welcome offspring to our woods.

Bittersweet vines and winterberry shrubs, both on Michigan's protected list, are doing well.

When the retirement complex started, shingle oaks—an unusual species whose leaves lack the usual lobes—were placed beside the health center. In 1991, we planted some of their tiny acorns, an experiment that has yielded a dozen trees now five and six feet tall.

In sunny, open places there are scattered clumps of Siberian iris, Missouri primrose, coneflowers, perennial pea, liatris, and hardy roses. In September, the entire area is a sea of goldenrods of five or six species.

Shrubby cinquefoil bushes add cheerful golden flowers all summer. Half a dozen viburnum species flower luxuriantly and three bayberry shrubs add interest. Witch-hazels of two species lend charm with unique wispy yellow and orange blossoms. I'm especially partial to plants that extend our flowering season, and the witch-hazels do this very well: native yellow trees blossoming into November and winter-blossoming orange ones opening in the ice and snow of February and March.

Hazelnut bushes have flourished, almost tree-size now. They bear dozens of tidy nut clusters. I kept wondering why squirrels didn't make off with them. On investigation, I discovered that many of the neatly nestled shells were perfectly formed, but completely empty. A mystery. What's needed to pollinate these tiny red star flowers in order to produce nut meats? Hundreds of long catkins shed golden pollen copiously for a week, but still we have empty shells.

Garlic mustard has not spoiled our woodlands as it has in so much of southwest Michigan, but spotted knapweed makes efforts daily to take over dry sunny edges.

Woodchuck holes are plentiful and deer are occasional visitors. We had pheasants for a while, but we've not seen them since reports of a fox surfaced.

Among nesting birds, we have tree swallows, robins, catbirds, song and field sparrows, goldfinches, mallards, downy woodpeckers, and red-winged blackbirds. Eastern bluebirds visit our boxes occasionally, but aggressive house sparrows chase them. Cooper's hawk, the killdeer, junco, white-throated sparrow, and brown thrasher appear from time to time.

We realize that our world desperately needs more trees to provide adequate oxygen supplies for expanding populations. Even with our efforts, we can't help but wonder what our woods will be like in twenty-five or fifty years. Will a beautiful and useful mini-forest be realized? Some of our oldest white pines are already bearing cones. Will our oaks have acorns? Will ginkgo and Cornelian cherry be fruitful? The year 2050 will hold the answers.

September 4, 1999

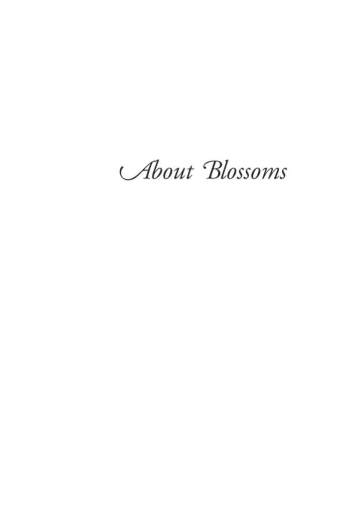

About Blossoms

Spring Treasures

Wнат ıs so rare as great white trilliums in flower as far as the eye can see? This choicest of blossoms with pure white petals flaring back has a chaste dignity all its own.

Have you experienced such beauty? Once in a great while, wildflower enthusiasts are privileged to find large areas with as many floral lovelies as could be wished for in one's wildest dreams. Great Smokies National Park has many such hidden places, but hikers can find them elsewhere, too.

Memory flashbacks bring me visions: thousands of pink lady-slippers in a Michigan state park; blue-eyed Mary drifting over hillsides at the Nature Center; vast tracts of Virginia bluebells, tinted rose and blue, nodding over a Licking County, Ohio, flood plain; marsh-marigolds sheeting a meandering creek bed, and forty acres carpeted with delicate pink spring-beauty.

It's this last location, a privately owned beech-maple forest, where I cherish a few hours of browsing each year on a bright, cool May day. At ten o'clock, the million (or billion?) spring-beauty buds are tightly furled, protecting pollen and nectar from overnight frost or possible showers. An hour later, with bright sun shining in the blue, blue sky, tiny candy-striped pink flowers are wide open and bees are busy everywhere.

Uncurling crosiers of lady, cinnamon, and wood ferns are delicate as can be: fuzzy, coiled pinwheels. Dutchman's breeches and bloodroot flaunted their charming white petals earlier and are now busily developing seeds before forest canopy leaves unfold, blocking off the sunlight plants require for photosynthesis.

Squirrel corn, with its strange little orange bulblet kernels under the mulch, is still in flower, looking like dainty white bleeding hearts. Insects have trouble pollinating it, and also its look-alike relative, Dutchman's breeches, because the very small entrance is at the bottom of the blossom and nectar is at the top. The roots—favorite food of small rodents—look like yellow corn grains, hence the name.

Amid golden marsh-marigolds in low areas, brave cold-defying skunk cabbages, their flowers faded; now they are lushly flamboyant green cabbages. Sunlight shining through two-foot leaves highlights intricate vein structures. Now is the time to note their locations to help you find the odd seeds in the marsh muck in late summer.

Some large-flowered trilliums are already turning the soft rose color of old age, but they are still dignified and beautifully proportioned. Leaves remain a rich, dark green until seeds are fully developed.

Yellow and blue violets are scattered throughout the woodland, along with several species of anemones. A few delicate wild sweet Williams, always latecomers, are just opening.

Along sunny patch edges, red-berried elder bushes are unfolding, their white floral cones promising brilliant scarlet fruits to come. Their berries are much loved by hairy woodpeckers, but shrub stems are a little thin for such a large bird; his efforts to get the fruit can be quite amusing.

Nearby are large, subtly colored, partly open buds of hickory trees. The dangling sepals' shades of mauve, yellow, and pink and their satiny, lustrous texture are almost breathtaking in their loveliness. What a good bud for time-lapse photography.

Dogwood leaf buds are partially open, but most of the flower buds were blighted in February's minus fifteen-degree weather. Beech buds' shiny golden cigars are still tightly furled, each one reflecting the sun's rays.

Soft green foliage of fragrant, fernlike sweet Cicely is everywhere. Clusters of petite dwarf ginseng's round, furry flower balls are almost lost in the lush spring woods vegetation. Old-timers dug this small plant for its edible tubers, fancying the pungent taste.

Open places in the path are scattered with tiny scarlet blossoms, dropped by red maple trees after their pollination was complete.

Harbinger of spring, hepatica, and cut-leaved tooth-wort, all early comers, are setting seeds now. Their flowers are faded, but their leaves and seed stalks remain among unfamiliar pairs of long-pointed leaves, which seem to speak of wonders yet to some. No. Later study reveals them as leaves of trout lily flowers, now long gone. As the plants mature, the characteristic small brown leaf spots disappear.

In *Chinese Encounters*, Arthur Miller wrote of a learned man named Lin Cheng, a retired official who loved landscapes and writing verse. He built himself a garden in the mountains, with a study. When his friends asked why he named it *Study Containing Spring*, he replied: "I like springtime the best. But it lasts only such a short moment. I want to retain it. I particularly want the inside of my study to be like a very long spring."

I think he had a good idea.

May 11, 1996

The Buttercups

BUTTERCUPS ARE BRIGHT YELLOW spring flowers well-known to most of us from childhood woods walking. Unfortunately, they're often strangers to today's children because roadside flowers now tend to be Eurasian weeds. Delicate meadow and brook blossoms, such as the half-dozen buttercup species found in wild parts throughout Michigan, can't tolerate highway pollution, road salt, mowing, and competition with tough aliens.

The buttercup family, the Ranunculaceae—named for *Rana* the frog who shares the same moist habitat—has about 100 representatives in colder areas of the northern hemisphere, including such springtime favorites as marsh-marigold and hepatica.

The most striking family characteristic is an odd one, the absence of petals which are replaced by colored sepals, often called tepals. Other field marks include alternate, compound, often divided leaves, many stamens, and several pistils.

Hepaticas, early blossoming representatives on undisturbed woodland hillsides, come in rose, lavender, blue, and white. On emerging as early as late March, they are swathed, almost hidden, in thick fuzzy hairs which—along with last year's leftover purplish leaves—serve as winter protection. The hairs stay on the stems, repelling ants who would steal nectar without pollinating the flower. Basal leaves are three-lobed and a liverish-red shade on the back. New leaves come as the flower fades and the sepals drop.

On a public trail, formerly a railroad right of way, observant walkers have found hepatica leaves with double the usual number of lobes, a fact sometimes absent from the literature. Round-lobed and sharp-lobed hepatica species are also found in about equal numbers. Sharp-lobed like alkaline soils, and round-lobed prefer more acid ground.

A doctrine of olden times claimed that medicines from plants whose shape resembled human body parts would be appropriate for curing illness of those parts. Therefore, the shape and color of hepatica leaves were thought to make them suitable for liver cures. The flower's name comes from the Greek *hepar* for liver.

Eastman, in his informative *The Book of Forest and Thicket*, reported that Chippewa Indians used hepatica root tea to treat children's convulsions.

Marsh-marigolds, or cowslips—close cousins to hepaticas—flower in calcareous fens and wet meadows shortly after spring peepers have started to peep. The shiny golden coloring matter on the five to ten sepals is so thick it can be scraped off; indeed, late frosts can make layers of it peel off, leaving nothing but gossamer tissue behind. These plants are light-sensitive, closing to protect their treasures on cloudy or rainy days when insects are not abroad. One wonders what kind of intricate mechanism in something so small enables them to be photometric. Broadly heart-shaped leaves are large, succulent, and shiny green. Interesting seed capsules, worth watching for, are arranged in a unique star shape whose segments often lie open after maturation, exposing their seeds.

Marsh-marigolds are one of that select group of plants which may have remontant blooming, a second period of flowering in the autumn when day lengths are the same as in spring—also a characteristic habit of violets and forsythia.

Columbine, another *Ranunculus* favorite, has seeds similar to marsh-marigolds, but they do not open quite so far. The five-parted papery pods are filled with many minute shiny black dots. The seed can be sown by wild flower gardeners as soon as it is ripe. Fertility of this plant is evidenced because shaded woods often offer you colonies rather than single plants. The scientific name, *Aquilegia*, comes from the long, curved flower spurs' resemblance to the talons of the eagle, *aquila* in Latin.

Showy blossoms of the columbine species, red with yellow face, dangle gracefully from eighteen-inch tall plants whose yellow-green leaves are finely divided into threes and are often decorated with white trails left by insect leaf miners. The thick perennial rootstocks last for many years and flower best in moist, less fertile soils. In rich ones, columbine tends to go all to leaves.

In 1949, one thousand botanists and wild gardeners were asked to list their twelve most favorite wildflowers. They rated columbine number seven and marsh-marigold number ten. How would you rank them?

Do you know virgin's bower, or wild clematis, another buttercup family member and a graceful, high-climbing vine that winds over acres of moist, wild land with its fine foliage and dainty petalless white blossoms? It flowers abundantly in September and is conspicuous in winter when silky plumed seed heads become snow chalices. Some people call these clusters of feathery hairs old man's beard.

Anemones are also members of the Ranunculaceae. Our regional representatives are the wood and rue anemones, and thimbleweed. Opening by mid-April, wood and rue species thrive in not too dry beech-maple woods. Petals are absent but sepals are white as white. Wood anemone's scientific name is *Anemone quinquefolia*, honoring its distinctive five-parted basal leaves.

Thimbleweed is named for its thimble-shaped fruit which may be an inch long and stays intact all summer. White flowers are similar to those of its anemone cousins but may be larger. The seed heads disintegrate slowly into soft fuzzy masses, not unlike those of cattails in the winter.

Scattered through woodlands during May, one may find flowers of red and white baneberry plants whose graceful compound leaves have three sharply toothed leaflets. Similar delicate clusters of white blossoms with one-eighth inch long petals and conspicuous stamens will mature into showy red or white berries depending on the species. White baneberry seeds, developing by midsummer, are china-white with a large blackish-purple spot giving them the common name of doll's-eyes. The fat white berries stand at right angles to conspicuous thick red stalks.

Red baneberry flower clusters are shorter and wider and mature into brilliant scarlet berries on more delicate stalks, berries so shiny they must have been varnished. Eating the acrid berry will produce very unpleasant digestive results. This red-berried form of baneberry is the more common one to watch for when exploring woodlands.

April 25, 1997

These Are My Favorite Things

T O WATCH THE DEVELOPMENT of a heavenly blue morning glory blossom from start to finish, from a narrow twisted beige cylinder to its well of intense saturated blueness dramatized by elongated points of a singularly perfect white star, is to be involved in a delightful adventure in botanical wonder, one which never fails to intrigue me. How could this flower be any more beautiful? It's always fun to attempt predicting which long pale bud is mature enough to open the next morning, to reveal its unexpectedly vivid color, silken texture, and striking pattern. Watching the slow unfolding, ever the same, starts me thinking about my favorite things in nature, those which bring me pleasure and inner satisfaction with the secret ways of the natural world—season after season, year after year, decade after decade.

A daffodil in all its phases is one of my seven wonders. The bulb, in hand, is dull brown with untidy tags of dried tissue clinging, giving no hint of inner secrets of beauty to come. Cut in half, it's just another onion. Add moisture, cold temperatures, and the passing of time, and one of spring's most charming marvels sprouts before our eyes. Supple, linear blue-green leaves emerge first, followed soon by a stiff stem, encased along the top in a semitransparent tissue. Slowly its fatter area bends over, a pale green outer skin peels back, and the glory of a graceful, golden blossom is revealed. Bulb catalogs show spellbound, even mesmerized, daffodil fanatics. But photography can't match the charm of reality: that perfectly formed, majestic trumpet with delicate fluted edge and graceful flaring backdrop.

I will long remember a spring foray into the woods outside Paris where many thousands of naturalized daffodils nodded gently in a breeze, a scene not unlike the one William Wordsworth memorialized. Did he say it all? I think the poet was charmed with the lushness of the overall spring scene, but I like to add my own delights: the perfection of silken tissue, the radiant intensity of color, the delicacy of enhancing dewdrops.

Daffodils are part of my rich childhood memories, reminding me of the importance of giving today's youngsters varied outdoor experiences. Our childish name for daffodils was "telephone talkers" after the trumpet-like wall telephone by our dining room table.

If I had to describe daffodil's essence in a single word, I think I'd choose loveliness. Too familiar a word? Maybe, yet suitable for the grace and simplicity of this blossom. Of the 250,000 flowering plants on earth, where do daffodils stand in your flower rating scale?

Another spring delight, again a true love since childhood days, is jack-in-the-pulpit, a quaint denizen of rich moist woodland soils. Jacks, Arum family members, come up as sharp points swathed in dark red membranes. Soon, one or two stout three-parted leaf stems emerge. Then the unique flap-like spathe, the pulpit, expands. The spadix, or jack inside its pulpit, is a club-like spike with tiny hidden flower parts, no petals or sepals, around its base. If fungus gnats do their part in pollination, a cluster of shiny green berries develops, becoming visible as the spathe fades. By autumn, seeds turn a handsome scarlet, the brightest sight on a forest floor. Jacks often grow in tight clumps where many seeds from a single head germinated. Left alone and undisturbed over the years, they will grow larger and larger, occasionally reaching over four feet and even having two pulpits.

About the time jack-in-the-pulpit is in flower, leaves on tulip trees are unfolding; that unique process is another of my favorite natural world miracles. I can't help wondering how such unique, efficient, and space-saving packaging ever came about. The child in me never ceases to be charmed by this magic packaging. Dark red winter buds at ends of twigs are shaped like duck bills or praying hands. When bud scales peel back in springtime, a tiny leaf folded over into a U shape is visible, slender stem on one side curled over to the blade, the leaf part. When this stem straightens, wishing to seek the sun, the upright leaf then unfolds down the mid-rib. Presto, there is the finished product in its perfect, four-lobed, top lobbed-off shape—truncated, the botanists say. At its base is another pair of duckbills which opens to reveal another lustrous bright green folded-over leaf, and so on ad infinitum. It's like unfolding thousands of chaise lounges. Tulip trees have other unique features such as the great heights to which they grow, straight unbranched trunks, charming bright greenish-yellow tulip shaped flowers almost hidden in lush June foliage, and unique light brown cones of seeds which tend to linger in upright positions all winter, turning the tree into a giant candelabrum. Bright yellow waxy autumn leaves are pleasing, too.

Of all these notable traits, the unfolding of leaves, guided by unseen regulations, pleases me the most.

Visualize a Michigan bog or a windswept arctic tundra decorated with hundreds and hundreds of fluffy, puffy cotton-grass plants standing above the surrounding vegetation and all swaying in the same direction. Ah, there's a scene to remember. This conspicuous plant, bearing dense cottony heads on two to three foot wiry stems, is a sedge, not a grass, meaning it has triangular rather than round stems and thrives in damp places with cold soils, either acid or calcareous. Neighbors in swampy borders of Kalamazoo County locations are sphagnum moss, leatherleaf, rosemary, tamarack, and blueberry. The more common cotton-grass species in southwest Michigan tends to be tawny, but the arctic species bear lustrous, pure white heads, golf ball in size— one of the few lovely things to be seen in barren rocky landscapes.

April 6, 1996

May at a Michigan Nature Center

THE LURE OF A BEECH-MAPLE FOREST in May is not the spectacular beauty of majestic, snow-capped mountains nor of murmuring seashores, but rather the beauty of evanescent, exquisite shapes and patterns, and of delicate pastels of a myriad inhabitants. Anyone who truly experiences a beech-maple forest floor's varied charms is hooked forever on its petite, ephemeral flower inhabitants. On our roadsides these days, forty percent of the flowers are aliens from Europe. In the forest, the same natives have been in residence for thousands of years. But timing is everything. The ephemerals seem to appear overnight, and if you miss them you'll wait fifty-one weeks to see them again.

It takes only a month for the natural world to cast off overnight freezing and thawing patterns and transform itself into uniform greenness. By May 31st, at forest edge, new leaves on eighteen-inch tall baby oaks may still be a surprising burgundy red, but the forest canopy is already a lush mass of same-toned greens. Gone are the many variations of beige, pink, tan, rose, lime green, and pale yellow that elm, maple, linden, and walnut buds flaunted at the beginning of the month. The oaks have dropped their masses of stringy male catkins, the pussy-willows have finished shedding golden pollen, and the hazelnuts are busy creating tidy shrouded seed clusters.

One of this season's most-loved charms, celebrated by bards since poetry began, is the luxuriant flowering of its shrubs and fruit trees. "Oh, to be in England now that April's here" wrote Robert Browning. Michigan orchards cry out for a Browning or a Vincent van Gogh to celebrate their lush beauty. Towns and villages are bright with golden forsythias and iridescent redbuds as they fling pastel beauty across our land. In low woods, one finds spicebush shrubs adorned with clusters of tiny bright yellow flowers. I hope we have enough bees left to pollinate every single blossom.

Along a bog boardwalk, leatherleaf's scruffy branches are bearing one-sided racemes of tiny white bells. Its dull but evergreen leaves have undersides dotted with rusty scales. This shrub member of the heath family grows there so luxuriantly in the acid soil that it threatens the existence of less aggressive plants.

Spring starts with blankets of some thirty species of delicate wildflowers strewn beside many trails. It's hard to choose favorites from such a rich and varied display. Remarkably petite pepper-and-salt-colored harbinger of spring, and mauve, pink, and white round-lobed hepatica's hairy-stemmed petals opened the show before the month arrived. Wild leek's bright green, broad leaves often cover large areas, only to die back completely and then surprise us with stalks of leafless white flowers in late July.

Scattered along stream borders in low wet, woods, tall clumps of leaves of early-flowering skunk cabbage are unfolding while the strange dark red spathes fade away. Did you know that wild turkeys have been found eating the newly emerged spadices of this plant and, in so doing, pierce the surrounding leaf structure so that it's somewhat lacy all summer?

What would spring be without wetlands sheeted with drifts of exciting bouquets of golden marsh-marigolds, or cowslips, as our fathers called them? Five to nine large shiny petals on sturdy green leaves ornament swamps, brooksides, and springy calcareous fens for weeks on end. I have seen them as early as March 12th, throughout April, and well into May. Half-dollar sized gold flowers sometimes appear again between October 7th and 24th, apparently when day length is similar to spring blooming time. What a delight to stumble across a few of them in full flower in a sunny October swamp.

Reflexed yellow petals nod on trout lilies, as do its long-stemmed seeds, by month's end. Wildflower books state that its rhizomes grow for seven years before having enough strength to flower. Do the bulbs die then? If they don't, you'd expect more flowering specimens among the large clones of flowerless, spotted, sharp pointed leaves. Or, like cousin trillium, does it take another seven years for the bulb to accumulate flowering strength?

Strings of delicately striped pale pink spring-beauties appear next, using energy stored in tiny bulbs twelve months ago. Its sweetly fragrant flowers keep stretching out, adding and adding new blossoms even when the first one has already developed a mature seed.

Too many species to count? Keep going—there may still be another shy beauty awaiting you down a beech-maple trail. Perhaps the most exciting array of all the ephemera is an expanse of the delicate blue-eyed Mary, a member of the snapdragon family. This delightful flower is abundant along the bank, thriving and spreading uphill in an ever larger area. Two white petals are united into an upper lip atop what appears to be two bright blue lower petals. Close inspection and careful handling will reveal a third blue petal concealed underneath, folded over two long and two short stamens, a most unusual arrangement. But watch the insects—they know the secret and go directly to the treasure house below the two bottom petals. This rare little beauty is a winter annual whose seeds germinate in autumn, ready to start up in spring and to be already in flower by early May. It is probably the only annual ephemeral and is found in rich deciduous woods in the southern part of Michigan. For me, it is the indisputable queen of our remarkable array.

Not often found, tall blue cohosh is so named because of its bluish stem, whose odd glaucous finish rubs off at a touch. Also, its berrylike fruits—which develop from small greenish-yellow six-pointed stars—are bright blue. These seed clusters on long stems turn black later, and are often identifiable above the snow cover in winter.

A second rarity is two-leaved toothwort, or pepperwort, whose single pair of opposite leaves is divided into three leaflets. Its more common cousin, cutleafed toothwort, has lance-shaped leaves cut into narrow sharp segments. Both species have the mustard family's typical four-petalled white blossoms. Two-leaved toothwort thrives in seepage areas and along streams.

Wild ginger's blossom is hard to find. The solitary, cup-shaped, maroon flowers hide under hairy-stemmed heart-shaped leaves. It is pollinated by the same flesh flies that like other dark red species: skunk cabbage, pawpaw, and red trillium. Attractive low-growing ginger plants spread rapidly, even in neutral soil, and make a splendid native ground cover in a woodland garden.

Everybody's favorite, the large-flowered white trillium, is scattered here and there, but the colony doesn't seem to be as dense as it was a few years ago. Hungry deer may have reduced it, or perhaps the storm loss nearby of an ancient beech tree permitted too much light to enter. Strange how even the sturdiest and most reliable of our woodland flowers are still finicky about their habitat. Where light, soil, and moisture are all to trilliums' liking, large areas often fill in solidly, creating unforgettable loveliness as the large white blossoms age gracefully into soft rose shades. If trillium stalks are cut, no nourishment can be sent down to the bulb and it may take many years for another flower to develop. The less common species of red, yellow, and nodding trilliums have often been introduced.

New and different species of always popular violets keep opening as the season moves along. The small, low, northern white violet and early purple ones are common as early as April 1st at the Nature Center. Downy yellow violets and common blue violets can be found scattered along woodland trails all through May. Long-spurred violet is less common, but quite easily identified by having leaves on flower stems, toothed stipules, a tiny face painted on beardless lavender petals, and—above all—the unusual long spur on the back of the lower flower petal. I've never found the beardless, pristinely white lance-leaved violet at the nature center, but in mid-May it's common along a bog boardwalk. The Haneses cite this species as being "frequent on the west side of the county in swamps and on sandy lake shores."

Throughout the month, ephemeral flowers blossom along the trails. By the time the brown thrashers are singing, Dutchman's breeches will have airy blue-green foliage peeking up from clusters of fragile, pinkish roots. The leaves make a fernlike setting for flowering stalks of four to eight bifurcated, inflated, crisp white pants, tinged faintly with pale yellow on the open lip. During their brief stay, the pretty, puffy sacs give off a faint perfume.

May apple nestles its white waxy blossoms at the axils of paired, lobed umbrella-like leaves. Tiny so-called apples, visible as soon as the flower unfolds, attain full lemon size by the end of July, and only a few last to maturity. This plant grows from aggressive rubbery poisonous root stocks, called clones, which may cover large areas. One feature that always intrigues me is that its flower bud—the size of a large pea—breaks ground first, followed closely by two leaf buds. Wouldn't you expect that the most important part of any plant would be spared such dangerous pioneering activity?

When the scarlet tanager is making his odd sore-throated robin call high in the tree tops, fungi that are the same bright red inside lurk down below him under matted leaves: the scarlet cups. They are exactly what the name implies: a shallow cup, one to two inches across and brilliant red, found growing on well-rotted wood. Usually, if there is one cup, there are at least five or six, so poke around a little in the decaying leaf matter hiding them.

Jack-in-the-pulpits are unmistakable, crisp and

green, sculptured as can be. They come up as sharp dark red spears that soon reveal one or two stems of three folded leaves. If two-stemmed, it will usually bear a jack flower with the familiar arching hood, or spathe, and its green spadix standing bravely upright inside. Georgia O'Keeffe observed this plant at Lake George one summer, and produced a stunning series of six studies of its charms. Some spathes may be lined with purple, some may be all green. Small insects enter the pulpit to pick up pollen in male plants, or to deposit it on the base of the spadix, which is all tiny pistils in female plants. Have you learned to tell a Jack from a Jill?

A stroll along paths reveals many blossoming delights. For example, you might see Solomon's seals—a sturdy plant group—members of the lily family, with flower parts in threes or multiples of three. So-called true Solomon's seal is tall and stately, with alternate, parallel veined leaves and greenish-white elongated bells dangling from leaf axils. The plumy false one arranges conical clusters of small white blossoms at the end of tall flower stalks. Foliage resembles that of true Solomon's seal, but the root stock lacks the seal-like scars that give the flower its name. In sandier areas, you might find a starry false one, a smaller plant with larger, starry white flowers, whose berries turn almost black.

There are colonial patches of rue anemones and groups of short-lived bloodroot's radiant white blossoms, carefully sheathed with sturdy lobed leaves that grow larger and larger after petal drop. Want to catch those seeds? Tie on a bit of nylon stocking so you don't miss the pod opening.

In the luxuriant drifts of Virginia waterleaf, early leaves are watermarked as the name suggests, but the later ones emerge unmarked. They come up early, but nodding clusters of pale pink to lavender fluted bells with long protruding stamens don't open until late in the month.

The last two major figures of the spring native flower show are the lavender petals of wild geranium and wild blue phlox. Take a close look at the geranium to learn why cranesbill is another common name. The central seed-bearing column, the crane's bill, is visible from the very beginning. Its dark green leaves are deeply cleft.

Wild phlox has lilac to lavender petals and grows one to two feet tall, liking shadier corners. The five petals may be slightly notched. Not as fragile as many of the woodland blossoms, it also thrives in home gardens, spreading gracefully as years pass.

Day by day, species by species, the ephemerals' moment passes. Beech tree buds lose their coppery sheen and show a fine fringe at the unfolding edges, fringes finer than a newborn baby's eyelashes. Old tissue-thin leaves, that stayed on all winter, are finally pushed off as new leaves unfold. Will this be a year that the beech bears nuts? It happens only once or twice in five years and, even then, many of the nuts contained in those prickly husks are infertile.

And so it goes, one lovely native species after another, all unattended all these centuries. Springtime trails are "A thing of beauty...a joy forever." And a caroling wood thrush's *ee-oh-lay* echoing among tender green leaves is the perfect accompaniment for a wonderful morning walk in marvelous, miraculous May.

April 29, May 6, 20, 27, 1999

Pollination

W<small>HY ARE SOME FLOWERS</small> so admirable in color and texture? Why do some have such intricate designs? Why do some have pleasant fragrances? Why do some secrete large quantities of nectar? Why do some, such as orchids, have complicated floral structures?

The answer to all these questions can be found in one short phrase: to aid in cross-pollination. This is the process of transferring pollen grains from the male organ, the anther, to the female factory, the pistil. After fertilization, the ovule begins to develop into a seed. Several vectors (from Latin, to carry) help to accomplish this.

Over time, plants have evolved many ways—sometimes tricky ones—to attract the creatures that will carry their freight to another plant so fertilization can occur.

An important vector, perhaps the most common but one we may ignore, is the wind. We know that the fine particles of common ragweed pollen appear out of nowhere every summer, causing so-called hay fever, which should truly be called ragweed fever. These invisible annoyers are picked up and borne to us on the wind. Most tree flowers and grasses deliver similarly. In June, white pine trees leave visible amounts of bright yellow dust on our windshields and sidewalks in copious amounts that can be shaped into miniature windrows. Why such generosity? Because winds are haphazard, particles must reach another plant of the same species, one that bears flowers and has female sex parts in the appropriate stage of development.

For instance, willow trees—also spicebush, sassafras, poplar, and ash—have flowers of only one sex on a given tree. The wandering male gamete has to find a tree of females with receptive flowers in order for fertilization to occur.

All common weeds and most early spring flowering trees are wind pollinated. Typically, these inconspicuous flowers have no calyx or corolla, no petals, which might impede the process. The all-essential flower parts, stamens and pistils, are present, albeit small and unobtrusive. Grasses and grains are similar. For instance, male parts of common corn are tiny green florets in tassels, up in the wind; pistils are lower on the plant. Their sticky, cottony stigmas, called corn silk, catch the pollen and ultimately make an ear.

Goldenrod flowers often are blamed for causing hay fever symptoms, but this amounts to character assassination. The pollen grains are too large, too heavy, and too sticky to be carried by wind. Only insects can be the transporters.

Insects, bees, butterflies, wasps, and beetles are the most commonly thought of delivery system. Plants have devised infinite ways to lure insects to perform the necessary transfer tasks. Some flowers use color as an attraction. Night-blossoming species, such as bladder campion, are white and have evening fragrance to attract night-flying moths.

Many blossoms, even those as small as spring-beauty, have decorative nectar guidelines on petals to show color sensitive insects where to go. Iris petals are heavily veined and have a golden carpet to attract bees. Tulip tree flowers have copious amounts of nectar and splash their bright yellow cups with brilliant orange spots. Bumblebees and ants are plentiful pollinators of tulip tree flowers.

Honeybees are the single most important carriers as they gather protein and oil-rich pollen masses to take to their homes. They fly miles to gather nectar but, interestingly, stick to one kind of flower per visit once they start sipping. A single trip may be more than half a mile long. Favored flowers usually are sweetly fragrant, sometimes pungent or fruity. Bees choose open or broadly tubular flowers that provide necessary landing platforms. Their favorite brightly colored flowers may be yellow, orange, white, blue, or purple. Bees are said to see red as gray, so they do not service red flowers. Orchard growers import truckloads of hives to provide enough bees to insure a good fruit crop.

But hummingbirds, another pollen carrier, thrive on red flowers, the brighter the better. Hummers, who hover wonderfully well, do not need landing platforms. They effectively extend straw-like tongues deep into columbine's and fuchsia's sweet nectar wells, incidentally transferring their pollen loads in their blossom-to-blossom darting.

Fungus gnats and flesh flies, attracted to rotting meat smells, pollinate skunk cabbage, wild ginger, and probably pawpaw.

Bats pollinate saguaro cactus and many tropical plants. Even snails do their share as they seek nectar and pollen to eat.

Except for eel grass in salt water, water rarely distributes pollen. Instead, this medium becomes important later when it's time to disseminate seeds.

Luther Burbank, a familiar name when I was a child, was nicknamed the Plant Wizard. A master of the complications of pollinating systems, he fertilized flowers by hand in laborious and meticulous fashion, creating many hybrids. His patience and deep knowledge of plant life are legendary. From the English daisy, the wild American daisy, and a pure white Japanese cousin, Burbank created the Shasta daisy, now a mainstay perennial of our summer gardens.

August 2, 1997

Blue

Blue is a curious word, often used without specific reference to coloring. Blue blood means coming from a noble or socially prominent family. A bluestocking is a learned lady. Blue chips are AAA type stocks. Blue laws were rigorous, morals-regulating rules in New England, promoted by bluenoses. Blue moon means a long period of time. Bluebeard married and killed one wife after another. Blue streak is the way some people talk or a special edition of a newspaper. When I was a child I was always intrigued to watch my mother pour bluing into the washer with her best white damask tablecloth.

Leonardo da Vinci puzzled over the cerulean shade of an unclouded sky. Jay Harjo, a Creek Indian, wrote of the "foreverness of blue sky." Susan Fenimore Cooper, daughter of James Fenimore Cooper, wrote of "the sky gleaming above in sacred blue."

Many native plants come in stunning shades of blue. Among the early spring flowers, the mass of blue-eyed Mary along the Beechwoods Trail at the Nature Center is a mecca for all wildflower connoisseurs. Most of them are stopped cold on finding the blueness of a delicate fringed gentian open to the sun, so intense the coloring, so perfect the architectural grace, so fine and delicate the fringe. Closed and soapwort gentians emerge blue but develop violet and maroon shading with age.

Wild iris's blue tones blend into the lavenders, as do many of the violets, but wild lupines, lovely pea-like flowers, are true blue. Blue-eyed grasses, members of the iris family, are identified by the way their leaves fold, not curl, around each other; their blue coloring is darker and quite intense.

Virginia bluebells are pink in bud, but the hanging trumpets are a lovely soft blue. In the suburbs where I grew up, bluebells were grown as garden flowers, complementing daffodils and tulips. The first time I saw them in the wild, there was a great expanse of them in a floodplain in Licking County. I've seen them elsewhere since but the breathtaking quality of that scene from more than fifty years ago is with me still. Porcelain-tissued bluebells, lush green foliage, and graceful dangling form characterize *Mertensia virginica*. The arctic species of *Mertensia*, called sea lungwort, is a low, matted plant found on ocean beaches, flowering even in ice and snow patches. Succulent foliage has a powder blue cast and the small flowers are as exquisite as those of our larger variety.

Forget-me-nots are a warm soft pale blue, contrasting with the intensely yellow eye. Great blue lobelia is a bold shade, set off by bright white stripes on lower lobes. Nodding harebell's delicate and deep-toned flowers are circumpolar, found in dry places the world around.

Hepatica blossoms are sometimes blue, but usually have a lavender cast as do the water-loving brook lobelias and pickerel-weeds. Blue cohosh is not named for its flowers but for the blue seeds which cling all winter.

Among alien plants, the cerulean blue colored chicory is the most beautiful blue under the sun, according to Teale. The ragged flowers open only to the sun for just a few hours, but the color is memorable.

I can't leave blue flowers without writing of the bluets, also called innocence or Quaker lady. A prairie flower, it is rare in my experience, but few blossoms exceed it in petite loveliness. Andrew Wyeth has a hauntingly beautiful drybrush watercolor of this tiny charmer.

Winslow Homer was endlessly fascinated with trying to reproduce the many shades of blue in waters of ocean and gulf. Lake Michigan's ever-shifting shades from silver to cobalt are worth an essay in themselves.

Ornithologists tell us that the blue of the blue jay's wing is an optical illusion. There are no such pigments in this bird's feathers. The color is due to fine reflective particles. Pound a feather with a hammer and the blue vanishes because the cell structure is destroyed. This strange phenomenon is also true of the wings of the eastern tailed blue butterfly.

But think of all the birds with blue in their names. Ralph Waldo Emerson said that eastern bluebirds carry the sky on their backs. The western and mountain bluebirds are even more vivid. Then there are the indigo and lazuli buntings, blue grosbeaks, and great and little blue herons. Kingfishers and swallows and nuthatches all wear some of this color. The blue-throated hummingbird, found only on our Mexican border, has an iridescent, powder blue throat, truly an amazing sight.

Do you like to eat berries that are blue? I do.

March 30, 1996

Color Me Yellow

UNLESS YOU WERE LUCKY this winter and had evening grosbeaks swarming your feeder, it's been a long time since you saw anything yellow. Suddenly, the male American goldfinches are yellow again, a sure sign of spring lurking around the corner. Dandelions will be exploding in sunny spots, and the eastern meadowlark on the pasture fence will flaunt his bright yellow breast.

Pollen dust from dangling hazelnut catkins will brush off yellow—an astounding 4 million grains of pollen per catkin. Soon, bold forsythia bushes and golden daffodils in yards and gardens will turn such areas into shining arrays. If it has been an extremely cold winter, only forsythia branches protected by snow cover will flower, creating a strange sight of blossoms only at ground level.

There can never be too many daffodils for me. I just wish they flowered all summer long, like dandelions. Their delightful floral design and graceful manner of gentle nods on the long blue-green stems keep them forever near the top of my top ten list.

Wordsworth enjoyed the naturalized expanses of daffodils in his beloved English Lake District and left us moving phrases lauding their beauty.

The dominant species of swampy areas and wet meadows in mid-April become delightful sheets of gold as colonies of floriferous marsh-marigold clumps do their thing, flowering with great ebullience. The coloring matter is so thick that late frosts cause golden layers to peel right off leaving behind a pale tan supporting structure. The half-dollar sized blossoms with bright yellow, glossy petals mature into starry, many-seeded whorls, unique designs worth watching for.

Another wet area denizen is the corky-barked spicebush shrub that sends out tiny round clusters of golden flowers. Particularly common in flood plains, it is decorative in the fall when its fruit is a brilliant scarlet.

Two varieties of yellow violets grow in woodland habitats: the smooth and the downy. These species are separated by the amount of hairiness on the stems, but still easily confused. The smooth form is more common, has more basal leaves, and flowers several weeks earlier than the downy, which has brownish lines on its petals and may flower again in fall when day lengths are the same.

On spring evenings, sunset clouds often have little peek holes filled with pale but rich lemon yellow tints.

In late spring, in wet areas where proud and stately European irises have escaped from gardens and become naturalized, their graceful golden blossoms rise above the marsh plants.

Yellow trout lily, also called fawn lily, adder's tongue, or dog tooth violet, flowers in beech-maple forests. Its tiny tooth-shaped bulbs take years to develop to flowering size. Thus, large colonies of sharp-pointed mottled leaves may have only one or two flowering plants. Yellow petals are strongly reflexed, exposing cinnamon colored stamens.

Isolated fen areas may have yellow bladderwort flowers open by mid-April. Strange and unique insectivorous plants, minute fragile root valves open and take in water. Then, special enzymes help the plant absorb the nutrients it needs from the aquatic insect bodies. Finally, the valves release the liquid and start over. Tiny pansy-like yellow blossoms will keep coming all summer.

The first yellow-rumped warbler of the year is always welcome with his flashy yellow, black, and white plumage. He's but the first of many of these crowd pleasers, most of whom will move on north to nest. The spring of 1996 was notable for unusually high numbers of warbler sightings because the cool wet weather had delayed foliage development. Trip lists of more than twenty species were not unusual.

Currant and barberry bushes in the woods have yellow flowers, often before their leaves unfold. Nearby on stream edges, several confusing species of buttercups will begin to open. Some are alien, a few are native, but all are lovely.

Wood betony has fernlike leaves and odd, closely-growing whorled clusters of tiny yellow or red flowers. Betonies are one of the species, like prairie smoke and trailing arbutus, which are dependent on soil fungi and, therefore, do not transplant well.

Once in a while, woods walkers will find bellwort's drooping flowers and their odd perfoliate leaves. And maybe even yellow trilliums in undisturbed woodlands.

Luxuriating in waste areas will be the alien wintercress, or yellow rocket, trying to confuse you with two different shapes of leaves.

Radiant sheets of gold covering damp areas are made up of golden ragwort, another species with two shapes of leaves and the region's only common spring-flowering member of the aster family.

When I was a child, one of our great backyard debates was whether or not, if we ate the leaves on the tasty yellow-flowering sour grass, the snake eggs on the leaves would develop into snakes in our stomachs. In retrospect, I'm guessing that the snake eggs were those foamy masses of harmless spittle bugs.

When the shy but magnificent yellow lady-slippers dangle their unique Cinderella shoes and spatterdock globes dot the little lakes, then we know that summer is here. The yellows of another spring have faded into history.

April 27, 1997

Orange

THE DICTIONARY SAYS that orange is any one of a group of colors that lie midway between red and yellow in the spectrum. We tend to define it as the color of the fruit by that name.

In nature, orange flowers are not so common as pink or yellow ones, but the brilliance of the saturation makes them exciting as they splash across a green meadow or ornament a ditch.

Butterfly weed is perhaps the quintessential orange flower, unique in shade, shape, and seed. Sturdy deep green foliage and red stems add to its cheerful charms. Well-named, the bright clusters found in sunny fields and road edges are favorite nectar sources for butterflies, large and small. Elegant swallowtails and backyard cabbage butterflies all sip from this gay blossom.

Although a milkweed family member, butterfly weed's hairy stems contain less milky juice than its cousins do. Native Americans used the erect, puffy gray-green seed pods in meat dishes the way we use green peppers. Folk medicine prescribed a cure for pleurisy made from its tough roots, giving it a common name of pleurisy root.

In pristine midwestern bogs in early August, one sometimes can find yellow-fringed orchids, misnamed plants that are truly orange. Nearly all orchids excite our admiration, but the stately bearing and delicate fringe of this rare and exotic flower are particularly notable. In a monotone green bog covered with sphagnum moss, leatherleaf shrubs, and tamarack trees, a single many-flowered spike of yellow-fringed orchid sets our mental salivas flowing copiously. By deeply fringing the edges of its beard, this flower flaunts its beauty to attract needed pollinators, without generating energy to make its petal landing platform of solid tissue. The conspicuous nectar spur is unusually long and slender, adding to its delicacy. Like all orchids in Michigan, this beauty is on the protected list. I cherish a fifteen-year-old memory of a small but pristine Indiana bog with some fifty of these elegant, fragile, orange stalks in full and glorious flower, a breathtaking sight.

Another orange flower of open summer wetlands or moist woodlands, but this one occurring in great abundance, is the spotted jewel-weed. Its translucent, frail stems support many two-parted blossoms. Take one apart to find the unusual separate cone-shaped spur. Blossoming over a long period, often until frost nips it, jewel-weed produces copious amounts of nectar which is said to be about forty percent sugar. Eastman's 1995

The Book of Swamp and Bog has an excellent explanation of this annual flower's various unique ways of assuring pollination and reproduction. The habit best known to most of us, the explosive projection of its seeds when fat ripe pods are touched, gives this plant another one of its common names: touch-me-not. There is a hypnotic fascination of feeling and watching the splitting, coiling, and hurling of seeds from small green capsules.

A number of native lily species flaunt orange flowers: wood, Michigan, blackberry, Canada, Turk's cap, and alien yet weedy common day lilies, all bringing gleams of color to ditches, fence rows, and meadows.

Spring flowers do not seem to come in oranges, oddly, but summer brings vigorous growths of trumpet vines covered with showy orange tubes as well as various bright and weedy hawkweeds.

By mid-August, hairy seeds on the tinker's weed, or horse gentian, are bright orange as are seeds of American bittersweet. Plentiful seed clusters appear on the mountain ash and turn from green to orange or scarlet. Unless eaten by birds, these ornamental fruits remain on the tree all winter. Stories are told of hungry cedar waxwings and American robins becoming drunk from eating too many mountain ash berries in spring after sugars have fermented.

Late summer means glimpses of orange on monarch butterflies, Baltimore orioles, blackburnian warblers,

American redstarts, and even chicken mushrooms. Bright leaves on sour gum, maple, and sassafras trees are all Mother Nature's way of forcibly reminding us of the beauty of orange.

September 6, 1997

Pale Pink

TWINFLOWER, A CREEPING PLANT of cool woods, is surely one of the daintiest and most charming summer flowers. Uncommon here, the paired, tiny, pale pink nodding bells, filled with short white fuzz, are fragrant. Much loved by Linnaeus, the Swedish taxonomist, it was named for him and for its northern habitat: *Linnaea borealis*.

Several other creeping woody plants with little pink flowers are characteristic of the heath family and are common in alpine and arctic areas. In recent summers, I've spent many happy hours botanizing three degrees south of the Arctic Circle on eastern Canada's Baffin Island, where these family members are among the few plants that really thrive in the difficult conditions. I've always been fond of pale pink whether in baby rabbit's ears when the sun shone through, in the blush of certain seashells, or in a just opened deliciously fragrant swamp rose. To find barren rocky tundra areas sheeted with small, shiny leaves, liberally sprinkled with pink flower bells of bilberry, mountain cranberry, bearberry, bog rosemary, or alpine azalea is truly a joy.

Pinkish blossomed pipsissewa—or prince's pine—is closely related to *Pyrola*.

Leathery-leaved trailing arbutus, another heath plant with ground-hugging woody stems and clustered pale pink flowers, which are both waxy and delightfully fragrant, covers large patches in the Upper Peninsula. It's only occasional in Kalamazoo County, but can be found in early April in the Grand Mere dunes, its charms often hidden under rusty-backed leaves. Dependent on mycorrhiza in the soil for necessary amino acids, arbutus cannot be transplanted successfully and is protected in Michigan.

Spring-beauty flowers are a delicate pink, accented by darker pink guidelines which help insects see where to go for their prizes. Some hepaticas are this pale hue above their furry leaf nubbins.

A pink tint is apparent in the bodies of newly-hatched birds, quite ugly creatures really, but showing promise of transformation into something more beautiful later. Adult roseate terns have a pinkish flush on their underparts.

Arctic, or bird's-eye primrose, likes calcareous pond shores, especially near the Mackinac Bridge or on Drummond Island, Michigan. Rising from a basal leaf rosette, the frail stem holds an umbel of flowers with pale pink notched petals, accented by bright yellow eyes.

Also on such pond shores, the gentian family has a

lovely species called rose-pink. In full flower, it's too rosy to qualify for this essay but, just opened, the pale pink contrasts with the center ring of golden stamens.

Showy lady-slipper's balloon-like pouch is flushed with pink, often turning rosy as the plant matures. The pink lady-slipper, or moccasin flower, is too intensely pigmented from the beginning to belong among pale pink wild things. Deptford pink, an alien from England, is also dark, but the woodland's graceful wild geranium, bearing its long cranesbill seed above five delicate petals, fits beautifully.

A common plant which can be pink, white, or pinkish-lavender is the daisy-like fleabane. Robin's plantain is a short cousin and its ray flowers are apt to be pale pink. The pea-like blossoms of trailing wild bean, found in swampy areas, are in soft shades of pale pink, mauve, and pale greenish-ivory. The swept-back comet-like petals of shooting star or the deep bells of Gerardia may be close by, often lost in sedge and grass jungles.

Among trees, pink dogwood comes to mind immediately. What a pleasure to drive to the Smokies during dogwood time. Homeowners in every village seem to vie with the next town for beauty of plantings. I'm partial to the profusion of pale pink blossoms on native prairie crab trees and have been working for five years at establishing a grove of them in the woods where I live. When a few of them flowered this year for the first time, it just whetted our appetites for the loveliness to come.

One of my small granddaughters likes all colors as long as they're pink. In preschool, she created a large pink dappled painting and titled it *It's Raining Pink and Red Strawberries*. A lovely thought! When we used to make hollyhock ballerinas, only the palest, gauziest single flowers were acceptable.

Sometimes during summer sunrise or sunset hours, an otherwise cloudless sky may have light pink gauzy garlands strewn around the entire horizon.

If you're lucky enough to be near a bit of prairie, you might find that marsh phlox, nodding wild onion, or, later on, low calamint, prairie milkweed, and field milkwort will be pale pink. Spreading dogbane has waxy, bell-like pale pink flowers with recurved leaves. Its paired, long slender pods are attractive all winter.

What can you find that's pale pink?

July 27, 1996

Some Summer Flowers

MOST WILDFLOWER FANS KNOW and love the exquisite woodland ephemerals that come and go quickly in April and May before leafing-out trees shut off light to the forest floor.

But what about summer field flowers? Because we haven't much open prairie left, opportunities for observation are fairly limited, but care and persistence over the summer will reveal some natural habitats. State parks and railroad rights of way often have native plants.

Unfortunately, old farm fields tend to be dominated by alien Queen Anne's lace and spotted knapweed, excluding all other species. These sturdy foreign plants—exotics—long ago survived civilization's pressures in Europe and Asia. Brought here, either intentionally or accidentally, they quickly established living quarters in areas too disturbed for native plant survival.

Native lupines, gentians, and lilies can't compete successfully with the aggressive mannerisms of the weed community: long flowering seasons, ability to withstand drought and flooding, toleration of soil variations and disturbance, imperviousness to insects and diseases, and production of incredibly large numbers of long-lived seeds.

Among surviving natives are members of the St. John's wort and cinquefoil families that flower from Midsummer Eve into August, sprinkling gold wherever they grow. Spotted St. John's wort, often found in semishaded damp places, is identified by tiny black glands on the undersides of both leaves and petals.

Lance-leaved and prairie coreopsis, daisy family members, live in sandy habitats and bear beautiful yellow flowers over long periods. Coreopsis is a good garden flower too, providing satisfactory table blossoms as well as creating favorite seeds for goldfinches. If you've once watched a goldfinch start at the bottom of the long thin stem and sidestep his way to the seed cluster at the end, weighing it down gently as he goes, you'll never be without it.

Spiderwort, with its grasslike foliage, a summer survivor, is frequently seen in roadside colonies. The large three-petalled flowers are an eye-catching intense blue or royal purple with accents of golden stamens, a striking combination calling for close up study to find the unusual purple hairs on the anthers.

Occasionally, these flowers are rose or even white. The largest colony of all-white spiderwort I've ever found was in sand dunes and was most attractive. But the stems were completely entangled in a healthy poison ivy ground cover, foiling a photographer's dream. A common name, widow's tears, refers to the brief period spiderworts are open, the petals dissolving by noon.

Flowers of the *Penstemon* genus of the snapdragon family choose sandy transition sites, moist or dry, and are always a treat. Inflated tubular flowers, pristine white or pale violet, are called beard-tongue because some stamens may end in tufts of hairs. Basal rosettes of shiny leaves sustain tall spikes with many horizontally oriented blossoms. One author thinks *Penstemon* blossoms look like musical horns ready to be played.

Wild roses of various species flower off and on all summer lending fragrance and color, and providing plentiful supplies of rose hips for winter bird food.

Members of the mint family are not spectacular in appearance, but are still quite charming, especially when viewed close up. Tiny orchid-like two-lipped flowers are usually numerous, tucked closely into axils of the leaves. Catnip, heal-all, peppermint, and the dead nettles are aliens, but water horehound and bugleweed, both with white flowers, are native. The tall white mountain mints, too, are natives, various species best told apart by differences in the paired leaves, which differ in shape, stem length, edge teeth, and hairiness.

The *Monarda* genus brings us lavender wild bergamot and yellowish horsemint, two sturdy mints in flower all summer, particularly along railroad rights of way.

Old-fashioned, always cheerful black-eyed Susan is perhaps our most reliable summer bloomer, even if it is biennial rather than perennial. It prefers rather sterile and somewhat acid soil and appears in both thicket and grassland.

Pokeweed is a large and vigorous native survivor often found in flower and fruit at the same time. Stems are reddish and the tiny blossoms lack petals although the white sepals resemble them. Tough, turnip-like roots produce leafy green shoots much sought after by greens gourmets. Thrush family members relish pokeweed seeds, so protect it where you can despite its phenomenal growth habit of eight feet in a season.

If you like swamp-stomping you might find pitcher-plants and iris early and jewel-weed and cardinal-flowers later. Also watch for the flowering of blueberry and buttonbush shrubs.

The most useful field guide, if you're intent on learning more about summer wild flowers, is still *A Field Guide to Wildflowers of Northeastern and Northcentral North America* published by Roger Tory Peterson and Margaret McKenny in 1968. Many other wildflower books are available, but often contain too few species, inadequate detail, and mediocre drawings or photographs. Peterson thought flowers would be simple to do after years of bird book trials and that he'd finish this one in a year. Even with the devoted help of McKenny, it took them six years to complete it.

July 19, 1997

October in a Bog

Do you know a plant called cotton-grass? If not, you have a fine opportunity to enjoy it in considerable numbers in southwest Michigan's West Lake Nature Preserve. In a ten-minute walk through an oak forest, you will go from a busy street to wilderness, into a true bog.

We walked this unbelievably lush wild area on a splendid mid-October day when airplane vapor trails decorated the bright blue sky in amazing geometric patterns, as if choreographed by some unseen genie.

We traversed this unusual habitat on a boardwalk, entering the area through a mass of blueleaf willows interspersed with tall swamp dock and large chain ferns. Annual herbaceous plants are losing ground now, withering and turning brown. We saw the beginning of an endless carpet of sphagnum moss which covers the bog as far as one can see. Soft pressure on lush moss pillows that surround leathery-leaved heath family plants reveals the depth and bouncy elasticity of sphagnum's water-filled, acid-loving masses. I think of moss as green, but this flourishing mat is rich in softly blended autumnal shades of pinks, rusts, chartreuses, and olive-green.

As I turn to survey the whole wide scene, a magnificent sour gum tree catches my eye. It is an artist's dream of flaring brilliant color; every shade of coral, raspberry, yellow, and scarlet is spread over the shiny surfaced leaves. Bright gold maples pale in significance beside this tree's regal bearing and variegated palette.

En route to the observation platform, the dominant shrub is leatherleaf. This acid-tolerant plant keeps its green leaves all winter. Observers will see high-bush blueberry, wishing for the season of their tasty fruits. Occasionally, there are wisps of bog-rosemary plants whose blue-green leaf surfaces are densely furred and have curled under edges to protect water content when plant roots are frozen and water is unavailable.

A surprising number of late mushrooms with brown and maroon colorings dotted the sphagnum mat. Here and there, tiny scarlet cornucopias of pitcher-plants were visible. The usual green coloring has vanished as photosynthesis stops. Sun shining through the pitchers reveals an intricate vein structure. We looked for faded umbrella-like flowers, which would stand well above insect-attracting leaves, but didn't see any.

Occasionally, cranberry's minute strands embroidered the mosses' surface with a goodly number of fruits in some places and none at all in others. How can so threadlike, so lacy, a stem support such a large berry? Cranberry's pink shooting star flowers in spring are one of the bog's delicate glories.

The outstanding autumn array in this bog is the field of tall waving cotton-grass, diaphanous round white masses, golf ball size, illuminated from behind by the low-lying sun. They nod above other plants, waving in the same direction with the breeze, and then drift back. I am mesmerized by the luminous rhythmic beauty of the scene, enhanced by sparkling blue lake waters beyond.

A few hard frosts will make the tamarack tree's delicate needles turn golden and then drop. We found them still green, a sturdy backdrop for the brilliance of the day. Bright red rosehips near the platform will cling until spring unless a hungry creature finds them. Bits of bog goldenrods and steeplebush and a few bog birch and poison sumac saplings grow along the walk. The presence of ten-inch young tamaracks is encouraging. They would not reproduce unless favorable conditions existed.

Cattails, water willow, and buckthorns with their blue berries are weedy intruders near the platform. I would wish them away, that the integrity of the bog could be maintained in its rarity. Their presence may indicate plant succession, buildup of nonacid soils—and perhaps—invasion of pollutants from the lake. We have found species of orchids here in May, a joyous occasion at any season. One hopes for their continued existence in this beauty-laden natural oasis.

October 28, 1995

196

Do You Know Fens?

I WALKED A FEN TODAY. What a glory! What a privilege! Just happened to be there at the peak of Ohio goldenrod's flowering. The modern comment would be rad or awesome or something of that order. I'll have to settle for heart-warmingly beautiful.

As I moseyed along on this gorgeous high skies day, looking for the entrance path, I noticed seeds from last year's flowers developing on the witch-hazel bushes, unusually lush vegetation. There were only a few flowers on the carrion vine and no great blue lobelias along the path. In the edge thicket a few ironweeds were showing rather anemic touches of their usually brilliant magenta. But when I broke through the glossy buckthorn hedge, I was stopped in my tracks by the stunning array of yellow spread in front of me.

The fen's staple, the shrubby cinquefoil bushes, sprinkled with bright yellow, five-petalled, open-faced blossoms, set the tone. This is a circumboreal plant found in calciphile soils, those with alkaline tendencies. But the hundreds of Ohio goldenrod plants in full bloom were the stars of this lakeshore. This is a softer, less aggressive goldenrod than many of its cousins, and is a specific indicator of fen conditions. The plants seemed taller than I remembered them, perhaps due to extra rains in May and June. Flat-topped, its long, narrow, light green, feather-veined leaves point upward instead of outward, giving it a special dignity all its own. There were several *Solidago patula*, the rough-leaved goldenrod, a taller, coarser plant, branched like an elm tree. It is found in other kinds of wetlands, but *Solidago ohiensis*—Ohio goldenrod—is faithful to alkaline soils found only in peat-laden fens.

A fen develops when a glacial till deposit is invaded by a river, or, as in this case, a kettle lake made by a glacier ice block, and thus, ground water that has been running through limestone based gravel is exposed. In a true fen, this water flows at the same temperature, with the same rate of flow, and the same chemical content for twelve months a year. I learned this with surprise one fifteen-degree winter day in this fen. The dog I was walking ran out on the frozen lake, yet I was standing almost ankle deep in water at the edge of the lake. In summer, the water seems very cold; yet it's the same temperature as in January.

On this August day the tiny, delicate flowers of the lavender Kalm's lobelia were everywhere, but hiding too far down in the dominant chairmaker's and spike rushes for their petite charms to be readily visible. Cobwebby swamp thistles, another fen indicator, were in full blossom. Their deep lavender flowers contrasted pleasingly with the prevailing bright gold. A few languid pink gerardia and numerous dense blazing stars—tall, purple, and stately—added more species and more color. A small white aster was just opening, here and there, a single white flower at the top of the plant. Asters are even harder to figure out than goldenrods, so it will remain nameless.

Several times, as I wandered through the congested area, I had difficult choices to make: should I joggle and perhaps spoil the state-of-the-art cobwebs of the flamboyant gold and ebony orb spider, or brush aside the poison sumac branches blocking my path? The creator of one web was perched right in the middle of its zig-zag escape route. Sun bathing? It usually stays down out of sight.

A pool dug out of marl long, long ago, where June brought us intermediate bladderwort flowers, was in midsummer dryness and devoid of flowers except a few seed stalks of pitcher-plants flaunting large flattened pistils. Because the pool was almost dry, the peat accumulations were quite apparent. The strongly alkaline nature of fens means that plant material doesn't rot, and generations of sodden peat accumulate.

Boneset, with unique jointed leaves and fuzzy white flower clusters, was in full flower, and a few tall Joe Pye weeds were turning pinkish purple. Mountain mints were past prime, but still shared their fragrance with the slightest brush of my fingers.

Two small ash trees near the lake edge were full of leaves as usual, but they never seem to grow any taller in this hostile-for-them setting.

Indian grasses as tall as I am were just maturing. Only one or two held the big yellow pollen grains that are so characteristic and so decorative.

Swamp milkweed's pink flower clusters were long gone, its unique green seedpods standing straight up.

I noticed only one marsh St. John's wort whose dark red buds seem out of place in this essentially gold and purple landscape. Its blossoms unfold only in late afternoon. Many botanists say they've never seen the open flower. This plant is mainly coastal, and it is at the western edge of its range in Michigan. Other species of this genus are yellow instead of this odd red that shades into maroon.

Here and there, a few deer tracks were apparent in the soft soil. Perhaps that explains the relative infrequency of nodding ladies-tresses orchids, well known here in previous years. I saw only four altogether, just opening. It's a charming flower with nodding white blossoms arranged in a double spiral twisted around the single upright stem. I never give up hoping that we might some day spot a small white lady-slipper. That exquisite species belongs in fens, too.

Grass of Parnassus has distinctive white blossoms

with delicate green veins and was scattered around. Don't deer like them? The rosettes of spoon-like leaves are such a delight when they first emerge in the spring. What can that be, you wonder, until memory clicks in.

Tiny spike-moss, *Selaginella,* I have usually found here wasn't apparent, but maybe I wasn't diligent enough in searching for this minute bit of green lace.

Two mute swans gliding on the lake were the only birds visible at midday. Bumble and honey bees were busy gathering goodies, and at least three species of butterflies were cheating Japanese beetles out of whatever they wanted.

In September, this fen will be at a visual feast stage again, when the lesser fringed gentians open their unbelievable blues to even bluer skies, and the poison sumac growing here so enthusiastically will be at its orange-to-red-to-scarlet flaming beauty peak. New England asters will replace today's blazing stars' purple, and big turkey foot grasses will be stretching up.

As I made my way out past red osier-dogwoods, covered with fruits, I felt refreshed and renewed to have experienced such beauty in this serene lakeside setting.

Late summer 2001

Henderson

Out and About

Of Love and Loss

And when the dawn-wind stirs through the
ancient cottonwoods, and the gray light steals
down from the hills over the old river sliding
softly past its wide brown sandbars—what if
there be no more goose music?

Aldo Leopold

WHAT KIND OF EMOTIONAL ATTACHMENT do you have
to the natural world and any of its many parts? What
long-gone place of happiness do you mourn? Would you
care if all the robins or all the violets suddenly disap-
peared?

Are you old enough to have experienced the passing of the magnificent American chestnut trees? How
did we commemorate such a monumental loss as that
of millions of graceful American elms? And now we may
be facing the loss of our flowering dogwoods. The de-
structive anthracnose—a disease caused by a fungus—
has taken them on both coasts, in the Great Smoky
Mountains and is currently found in Illinois. How will
we mourn such devastation?

Does it bother you that garlic mustard plants are
dominating our woodlands, crowding out bloodroot

and columbine, trilliums, ferns, and jacks you've loved since childhood? How do you mourn their loss? Develop a meaningful ritual? Write a poem? Send letters of remembrance to your friends? Make sketches to keep the memory fresh in your mind's eye? Build a monument saying, "Here grew my favorite wild flowers. R.I.P.?"

How can we openly, creatively, express our sorrow for loss of a tree, a plant species, a beloved natural setting? Should we have a remembrance day for the trees lost in a downtown park in Kalamazoo's worst tornado?

Processes of natural evolution are taking away—and adding—species every day, and man's activities, coupled with the world's burgeoning populations, are accelerating the pace of the taking away. How much do we care for what we are losing? How do we grieve when we lose earth's nonhuman life? When our friends die, we put their bodies or ashes in special places we can revisit, we have wakes and funerals, place memorial flowers, write letters of condolence, lower flags to half-staff, or construct statues and monuments as was done for the passenger pigeon. All of these actions are to honor human friends we have lost, to express our respect and emotional bonds, to help us accept the death.

How can we openly, permanently express our sense of loss for favorite woodsy places, for long-admired great trees, for mountain forests laid low by smelting plants and acid rain, for plant and animal refuges destroyed by drilling rigs? Do such losses spur us on to more serious conservation efforts? Do we take the need for careful stewardship of wild areas more seriously?

Many years ago, when Mono Lake in California was still being drained below maintenance level in order to supply Los Angeles' endless need for more and more water, we were on a birding trip hoping to see some of the thousands of phalaropes that stopped there on migration. But the water level was too low and the birds were absent. At supper that night our veteran leader, who had been to Mono Lake many times, sat in the corner of the cafe booth silently weeping, unable to stifle her grief over the loss of this fascinating species. I never will forget her genuine sorrow. It was the kind of desolation I would feel were I never again to hear the haunting *ee-oh-lay* of a wood thrush echoing through a shady woodland, a sound which evokes every wild and lovely place I've ever known, a feast to my ears and my sensibilities.

What are your happiest memories of long-gone natural history objects, stored away in odd corners to be retrieved at your call? What wild flowers still blossom in your heart? Is that memory enough? What would be an appropriate way to express your bereavement, your sense of loss, to commemorate a beloved place now under concrete?

I admire scientists' willingness to admit they have feelings of emotional warmth about the organisms they study. Surely, Carson's writings—produced under severe stress of family problems and recurrent cancers—are a philosophical statement about the sea and its organisms. They are also a profound statement of affectional respect, her ecological love, if you will.

In my favorite *Orchids of Indiana*, Michael Homoya breaks into detailed paragraphs of scientific data with, "The orange-fringed orchid is undeniably a spectacular organism. During the dog days of summer when few other plants are in bloom, *Platanthera ciliaris* stands ablaze in glory, putting on an unforgettable display." Such is the kind of love that generates sincere grieving.

The loss of the ecosystems of the rain forests of British Columbia and Central America is not only a blow to the biological diversity of our world, but also a reduction of beauty and wonder in our lives. How can we express this feeling of being bereft? How do you conduct a personal cycle leading to recovery from mourning for inanimate objects?

Scientist Edward O. Wilson, who coined the term biophilia—love of living things—states his belief in our inborn need to connect closely with outdoor life for our own emotional and physical health, a need to celebrate nature. This being true, how do we grieve constructively when our connection is broken by destruction of that which we love?

A host of distinguished authors from Henry David Thoreau through Edwin Way Teale, Ann Zwinger, and

Aldo Leopold have told us of their manifold joys, their personal renewal in encountering nature. Who has guided us in devising a ritual, a ceremony, that would direct our laments?

The great taxonomist and botanist Linnaeus said, "If a tree dies, plant another in its place."

To experience death is to be mortal. It's a fact about living which we all have to accept. That's not to say, however, that losing a cherished tree or flower, even a bog, doesn't hurt, doesn't leave a void calling us to find ways to express the feeling. Sharing a sense of loss with others is often comforting.

In her 1995 Sierra Club book, *The Ecology of Grief*, Phyllis Windle suggests—in relation to the AIDS names quilt—that ecologists could create "a quilt of our own, with panels to celebrate the species we have loved and lost." Such handiwork could easily be an article of great beauty.

Perhaps setting aside a memory time to think about favorite woods or beaches now gone will be a healing recognition of their importance in your life.

November 8, 1997

Eds. Note: The author mulled this article over, off and on for seven weeks this summer, as she looked out over the Arctic's Frobisher Bay. Pitcher poses many questions to which she has no answers.

World-filling Light

Light effects at sunrise and sunset have charmed artist and poet as long as there have been artists and poets. Each and every passing moment brings subtle shifts, changes in tone, increases or decreases in luminosity; clouds and sun play tag with the horizon. "Where is that patch of pale aqua? It was there seconds ago." "What happened to that streak of chartreuse? It was almost the shade of the eerie pulsations of northern lights." "Will I see a green flash as the sun disappears tonight?"

In December, the sun moves farther and farther south increasing our hours of darkness, making each hour of light more precious. Sunsets seem more brilliant, more radiant in their splendor, on the few days they are granted to us, in welcome contrast to prevailing overcast hours. Moments of afterglow are more precious, reflecting the beauty that fades so quickly.

Rabindranath Tagore, the east Indian poet, wrote: "Light, my light, the world-filling light, the eye-kissing light, heart-sweetening light."

If you leaf through a portfolio of Jan Vermeer's paintings, or one including works of several French impressionists, it's immediately clear how hard painters work to tell us about the beauty of light.

Claude Monet kept many paintings going at once, working on individual ones only a few minutes each day—when light was the same as it had been the day before—so careful was he to keep detail and feeling accurate. Rembrandt van Rijn made his oil portraits unusually dark using bright shafts only to illuminate special details. The German poet, Hermann Hesse, wrote of "the eternal game of lights and shadows."

Physicists who study optics, and many astronomers, spend their lives exploring properties of light, the effects it produces, and such special phenomena as prisms, rainbows, quantum theory, rings around the moon, odd reflections, and even sundogs. I find sundogs particularly interesting and wish they were more common. I've spotted them only three or four times—a brilliant fragment of a rainbow, usually found on extremely cold days, peeking through cloud cover, along the parhelic circle around the sun.

Winter brings unique effects. On a warmish day, snow cover is just a white blanket, but on cold sunny days when every bit of moisture in the snow crystallizes and reflects the light, the effect dazzles the eye. e.e.cummings phrased it, "now the eyes of my eyes are opened."

Early one November morning, after a heavy wet snowfall, the usually monotone-colored bog displayed a dramatic appearance. Needles on tamarack trees had turned a warm golden-beige shade but hadn't dropped. Spangled with snow crystals at sixteen degrees, the rays from the low-lying sun turned each golden tree mass into glittering magic; the surrounding snow reflected the glory, creating a vision best described by the word effulgence. Half a dozen mallards and a statuesque great blue heron busied themselves in the surrounding open pools, oblivious to the uniquely lovely landscape.

Existence in arctic villages during long dark winter nights is truly dreary. Christmas stars on roofs remain illuminated twenty-four hours a day for months, just to add a bit of cheer to the prevailing gloom. Such use of electricity is limited because of the north's total dependence on oil supplies. Ice conditions, varying from year to year, can prevent the all-essential tankers from making scheduled August deliveries, but the cheer the illuminated stars bring justifies the use.

In Yellowknife, Canada, it's strange to see the sun just barely visible above the horizon at ten o'clock on Christmas morning, with thermometers shivering at twenty below zero and Audubon bird counters unidentifiable in their many layers of clothing.

Light is life-giving. Visualize the most lush beech-maple forest you know as it would be on May Day—every inch of the floor alive with delicately colored spring flowers. And three weeks later, all flowers are gone; it's a virtual nothing and will remain that way for nigh a twelve month. Why? The explosion of foliage in the treetops is so great that all light is blocked from the forest floor. The delicate ephemerals quickly finish storing essential food for their long period of quiescence. They then retire from the scene, only to emerge again as hours of daylight lengthen in April. Ernst Haeckel, a German scientist, wrote, "The whole marvelous panorama of life that spreads on the surface of our globe is, in the last analysis, transformed sunlight."

Do you remember your grade school science plant experiment in which you planted bean seeds in jars? You deprived some of water, some of nutrients, some of heat, some of oxygen, and some of light. All plants were depauperate, but the ones in the dark were poorest of all. And when you restored them to optimum growing conditions, then you studied phototropism, the way plants grow toward the light.

December 7, 1996

Early, Early Mornings

Each day the world is born anew.
James Russell Lowell

WHAT IS IT ABOUT THE SUNRISE hour that makes our outdoor world so alluring to nature lovers? Some of my most cherished memories are from very early morning times spent in the out-of-doors.

As teenagers in summer camp, my friends and I pulled our cots out of our tents at night, placing them together in a congenial row in the meadow. The star-strewn sky undimmed by city lights was our only roof. By morning, our blankets were dew spangled—even soaked. We were loathe to break the spell of the freshness, the mesmerizing monotony of the mourning doves' calling, the light rays creeping through the junipers making shadows shorter every minute. No human voices, no hustle, just serenity and peace pervaded the meadow. One by one, as heads lifted, they promptly ducked back into the covers, reveling in the deliciousness of the moment.

On a Mexican visit to Guaymas on the Gulf of California, the world so bright—as only tropical coasts can be—I went out early, curious to see some new birds. But I did not see any. No. I only heard them. The memorable cacophony of that dawn chorus held not a single familiar note. The grunts and the squawks and the shrieks outweighed any possible melodic notes in both number and volume. I did enjoy the large bright yellow trumpet flowers on the allamanda vine, and on the way home we saw white-necked ravens by the side of the lane.

When I was doing bird research in a fifty-five-acre post-fire tract in a wooded section of Indiana Dunes National Park, my protocol routines called for early morning walks in the area as frequently as possible. I'd drop off the country road into the low, narrow woods path and was immediately immersed in cool damp air, in airy soft pillows of misty fog lying a foot or so above the vegetation. Every flower or branch that my shoulder touched shared its dewy freshness, whether I wanted it or not. But the stimulating fragrance of the vegetation of that clear, clean air was so energizing it was worth bottling, if such were possible. Here, in spring, I could sort out the towhee calls from the great crested flycatcher's, the flicker rattle from downy woodpecker whinny, catbird meows from ovenbird chants. For a few years after the April 1971 fire, I had golden-winged warblers and yellow-breasted chats, both birds rare, beautiful, and also distinctive singers.

In Door County, when I was up and out early one

morning, before The Clearing students had come to, I found a dappled newborn fawn on the front hill, right beside a colony of yellow lady-slippers in full bloom. What a delight! The doe must have been close, but she didn't show. I sat down a hundred feet away and just inhaled that June morning.

Another early morning in Door County, one of my students and I were making a quick bird walk, moving along rapidly, hoping still to be on time for breakfast. A strange bird call in the field behind us made us turn around, and, to our amazement, that area was full of hundreds and hundreds of hummock spider webs all glittering with sun struck dew crystals. Walking towards them, they were not apparent down in the brush, but backlit by the rising sun they were magical. The bird call was forgotten as we were spellbound by the unexpected magnificence. Ellen and I are friends forever, privileged to have shared such an exquisite sight together.

An early-in-the-day beach stroll, before the sun got too hot, took place on Pawley's Island, South Carolina. This walk netted me the only really perfect seashell I've ever found. I've earned the Sanibel hump gleaning for shells in Florida several times, but never found as perfect a one as that olive shell from the barrier beach. It still sits on my curio shelf. It was a hurricane summer, and there were drifting sugar cane plants blown up from luckless places. I looked for insect or animal life in the wreckage, but to no avail.

In a poetic mood I once wrote of favorite August dawns:

> Come with me to August dawn.
> Ere first light barred owl called, deep, deep.
> Now woods are silent save for untiring crickets,
> Hushed is the spring dawn chorus that lifted my heart.
>
> Silvery moon sickle hangs low in the east.
> Soon 'twill be vanquished by a fiery sphere.
> Cotton-wool cloud puffs float aimlessly
> Await momentary incandescence.
> Spectral ground mists shroud dune crests and
>   dew spangled fields of grass.
>
> The crickets slow; a far cardinal whistles thrice.
> The east explodes with light
> The nascent moon dies.
> The day is born.

But winter morns have special charms, too, if you dress comfortably for the challenge. When we spent Christmas at Grand Canyon I found neat, precise tracks in fresh snow on the canyon rim path. Obviously one of Santa's reindeer had come looking the night before. The canyon itself was mysterious with swirling masses of fog wandering around. My almost grown-up grandson forgot his new dignity and made an angel in the snow. Needless to say, the rest of us did likewise.

Another wintry morning I remember was an Audubon Christmas count day in Indiana Dunes, when we wakened to twenty-six inches of heavy, wet new-fallen snow. The previous year, our count had had several hundred red-headed woodpeckers, more than any other tally in the country, and we were hoping to match that record. End of dream. My yews and white pines were beautiful in their crystal mantles, but my bird feeders were unrecognizable mounds and my 200-yard driveway impassable!

On another never-to-be-forgotten morning—at minus twenty-five degrees—the first black-capped chickadees dashed into snowy feeders with large frost crystals sticking up all over their little backs. The formations—precipitated from moisture-laden, very cold air—glistened in the early sun rays.

Some cold mornings, I'd walk over to Lake Michigan to watch the big orange sphere illuminate heavy cloud masses above the grayed lake. Reflected rosiness in northern and southern skies added pizzazz to a cold snowy expanse. If the sun really came out, rays would dance on the unique formations of icicles, sand, and snow that storms created on the ice collar protecting the beach, collections never the same two days in a row as sun, sand, wind, and water played their endless magic games.

One windy and chilly morning a snow bunting in somber winter dress flew just ahead of me for half a mile down the beach, fluttering a bit, then dropping down over and over to pick up some imagined morsel. He and I had all the beach, all the sky, all the lake, and all the dunes for our very own.

In summer on faraway Baffin Island's arctic shore, I liked quiet, early morning summer walks downhill to Frobisher Bay to see what the tide was doing. All-night light conditions and forty-two-foot tides at Iqaluit were unique in my experience, and I never tired of seeing daily differences in light and tide levels. I liked to stand absolutely still at water's edge watching that immense volume of water move past me in absolute silence, never hurrying, never slowing, just creeping, creeping up or down the beach in almost imperceptible never-ending movements. Walking the wrack line was fun too, to see what the tide left in the way of seaweed, feathers, or old caribou bones. Clumps of beach sandwort sheltered colonies of sea *Mertensia* of delightful charm, pink in bud and blue in flower, just like our Virginia bluebells. Low and matted, high tides could wash over them easily. Ravens, white snow buntings in summer dress, longspurs, and wheatears added to pleasure of early jaunts.

October 21, 2000

Intriguing Words

UNUSUAL WORDS ARE FUN to think about and would-be botanists find new ones frequently. I never studied Latin and Greek, the basic languages for scientific terminology. My anemic French and German don't help with a word like OBDIPLOSTEMONOUS. There's no familiar sound. The word means a blossom where one set of stamens is opposite the petals and a second set opposite the sepals. Pronunciation is something else. If you follow the usual rule of accent on the second syllable, you get a mouthful of fluff. Accenting the third syllable works.

Ornithology is a familiar term meaning study of birds. *Ornith* is Greek for bird and ornithophile means bird lover, but who could guess that ornithophilous describes a flower pollinated by birds?

Those who struggle with osteoporosis and go to osteopaths may know that the stem oste is from the Greek *osteon*, or bone. Osseous means bony and botanists say that ossiculus is a peach pit. To be pestiferous is to be annoying and botanists say that if you're petaliferous, you have petals. If you'd rather be tuberiferous, you'd have tubes at your base.

If you tell a seasick person that he is pisaceous, meaning pea green, you would not be thanked for your candid observation. If you're pisiferous, you bear peas.

Plant Identification Terminology by James G. Harris and Melinda Woolf Harris lists ways of being a leaf:

> acerose, awl-shaped, gladiate, hastate, cordate, deltoid, lanceolate, linear, elliptic, ensiform, lyrate, obcordate, oblong, perfoliate, quadrate, obovate, orbicular, reniform, rhombic, oval, ovate, rotund, sagittate, pandurate, peltate, spatulate, and subulate.

One could create rhyming poetry with such an assortment. Try reading the words rapidly, in groups of three.

Plant dictionaries offer delightful reading ranging from Aaron's rod to zygopetalum. Scholars of word origins know that the name of a perennial named cymbalaris comes from Greek *kymbalon*—a cymbal—and refers to cymbal-shaped leaves. Golden Tom Thumb cactus has golden spines. Hottentot fig and cobweb houseleek suggest fertile imaginations. Devil's backbone, devil's claw, and devil's tongue are folk names. *Doronicum pardalianches* means strangling leopards and, because it is poisonous, is appropriately called leopard's bane. Maids of France, elk's horn fern, false mermaid, fiddler's trumpet, flame of the woods, flower of the western wind, and Jupiter's beard prove that botanists can be fanciful.

One of my philosophy professors had the largest vocabulary of anyone I've known. Each lecture brought a long list of words to look up. My favorite was eleemosynary, meaning supported by charity. Asked how he developed such an assortment of words, he replied that he read dictionaries for fun as a child, turning to given pages, perhaps all that included the number five, and then hunting for new words.

On a birding trip, someone asked which word in the English language had three consecutive sets of double letters. I won't tell you the answer.

March 27, 1999

Indian Summer

Here it is again—one of those peaceful and dream-like Indian summertimes, with a day so balmy we'd like it to replicate itself for weeks to come. How can a day be so delightful? The sky, the air, the breeze, the temperature—all just right! The creek, the blue lake yonder, the woods—each little part of our landscape is at the peak of seasonal perfection. Even if I could, I wouldn't change a thing; I'd just stop the clock.

A red-bodied dragonfly hovers, alights, spreads gauzy wings out flat, ignoring a nearby mourning cloak butterfly that will soon seek shelter under loose tree bark, to winter there as an adult.

A blue jay, volunteer policeman of the woods, breaks into the quiet, screeching out a warning; not a welcome sound, perhaps, but his indigo blue and white costume is certainly eye-catching. A chickadee's more modest and confiding notes match his tidy gray, black, and white garb.

Red maples are scantily clad now, but the brilliant low sun shines through their scarlet filigree, creating a glowing memory, ready to lift our spirits when a thirty mph gale off Lake Michigan sends freezing sleet sheets every which way.

In one of her poems, May Sarton asked why light shining through autumn leaves is so magical. I can't answer her question, just affirm the sensitivity of her observation.

Flowering dogwoods, leaves shading gently from brilliant reds to ruddy wine, hold a few scarlet seeds missed by hungry migrants. Birds relish their high fat content, richest of all seeds.

Many oak leaves still rustle on high. Stiff dry ones on the path appear varnished and are just right for nostalgic scuffling. Gone is the fragrant leaf fire smoke of yesteryear.

Staunch and sturdy, thick-trunked walnut trees stretch bare dark limbs skyward. The ground beneath is littered with whiplike stalks from long compound leaves, mingling there with round yellow-green nuts. The volume of seeds dropped from giant old walnuts boggles my mind. What if all plants were so fertile? What if squirrels didn't find delight in gathering and eating them?

Norway maples still in full leaf have turned golden yellow, their brilliant mass punctuating the lightly veiled but cloudless cerulean blue sky.

Tamarack trees' summer greens have faded into soft orangey-beige. Some years, needles turn pure gold before dropping. Charming little rosebud cones may stay all winter, ornamenting bare branches, proving that tamaracks are both deciduous and coniferous.

Along the shady woodland lane, bottle-brush grasses—nestled among barely yellow thin-leaved cone-flowers—are holding onto their unique long, stiff awns. The only real flower colors lingering now after several truly frosty nights are the purples of two alien plants, spotted knapweed and heal-all.

Do you know blue-stemmed or wreath goldenrod with glaucous, or waxy coated, stems and a tuft of yellow blossoms in each leaf axil up the stalk? Well, the flowers have now become charming mothball-sized fluffs at every axil, a most graceful arrangement.

As I leave our serene woodland, on such an ideal Indian summer day, flashes from the monotone winter plumage of American goldfinches flying by remind me that this tranquil ambience will fade, and I must enjoy its essence while I may.

October 7, 2000

Signs of Autumn

A<small>RE MORNINGS SEEMING COLDER</small> and darker? Is the sun setting ever earlier, cutting short those lovely quiet evenings? Have you noticed that the greens of tree and shrub foliage have darkened, all appearing to be the same deep shade, and that the soft paler chartreuses and pea greens characteristic of summer are disappearing? Are nighthawks flocking? If you know the whereabouts of a sour gum tree in a damp spot, perhaps its red and orange colorings are already visible.

Needles of white pine trees that have been attached for four or five years are turning brown and dropping. This discarded, soft abundance is amazing. Even if they are not fragrant, like the sweet-smelling balsam ones, they make good strawberry mulch.

The more obvious signs of autumn are not yet apparent, only subtle daily changes in quiet places. Corky layers between leaf and twig are thickening, and even now a strong wind means falling leaves.

Pokeweed—or pokeberry, pigeon berry, or inkberry—has reached its maximum height of ten to twelve feet, amazing growth to rise from nothing in one season. Along hedgerows, or in low rich ground, poke's generous crop of shining purple berries provides banquets for robins, flickers, woodpeckers, towhees, grosbeaks, and migrating thrushes. Long ago, when we all hung our laundry out to dry, this plant wasn't allowed in the garden because the purple bird stains were permanent. Indeed, Indians used it to make red and yellow dyes. The heavy coarse stems now have a reddish cast, and the drooping, corduroy-ribbed stems hold clusters with ripe fruit and new buds at the same time, an unusual pattern.

Examined closely, you'll see that poke's tiny flowers have no petals, just greenish white sepals which make neat lace doilies for the intricate ten-celled button-like seeds. Smooth-edged leaves, sometimes a foot long with prominent veins, emit a strong odor when crushed. The large root is poisonous, but young shoots often are eaten like asparagus.

Red squirrels are busy storing jack pine cones and black walnuts against the winter cold. Such sapient thriftiness. Last spring, I found an egg-sized clump of about forty sprouting black cherry trees two inches high that, I'm sure, represented an uneaten chipmunk or squirrel hoard.

Wooly bear caterpillars are much in evidence, all brown or banded brown and black, a certain sign of autumn to come. Great favorites of children, they roll up tight when disturbed, but eventually unroll and proceed on their way. These caterpillars hibernate in their thick fur coats and emerge from cocoons as Isabella moths. On Baffin Island, five degrees south of the Arctic Circle, where fifty below temperatures prevail for weeks, I've seen wooly bears in June. Where can they hide in January?

Pond borders and damp places now are sporting great blue lobelias in their full array, a stunning shade of blue with contrasting white stripes. Note how oddly this flower is arranged with its stamens apparently forcing their way through upper lobes. Tiny look-alike cousins, the bog or Kalm's lobelia, is in flower in springy sites amid grass of Parnassus and budding fringed gentians. Another lobelia, the most eye-catching and regal of all, is the brilliant scarlet cardinal-flower. In undisturbed swamps, stalks may grow six feet tall with as many as seventy-five blossoms. Cutting fading stalks before seeds develop promotes growth of leafy basal shoots, ultimately increasing the patch.

If the season is wet, mushrooms are everywhere in every color. Sometimes the most beautiful are the most poisonous, but the wide array of patterns, shapes, and tints is one of late summer's most fascinating wonders.

Cattails are maturing in shallow wet areas among milkweeds, autumn willow, and swamp asters. Can you tell the wide-leaved species from the narrow-leaved by whether male and female parts are touching or separated on the stem? Did you know that University of Michigan botanists say there can be as many as a million seeds on one single plant? Other scientists say 300,000—take your pick. Either way, it's a reproduction miracle. These plants are extremely prolific, both with pollen earlier and seeds now. Take one tail apart and study the tiny fluffy components, used by native Americans for bedding and for lining mittens, moccasins, and even the papoose carrier. Instant disposable diapers.

September 7, 1996

Is There Black in Nature?

A CENTURY AGO, a frequent discussion topic among French impressionist painters concerned the color black. Was there black in nature? Should black appear in their paintings?

If you browse through *One Hundred Flowers*, a magnificent portfolio of Georgia O'Keeffe's works, you will see that hue frequently used in her paintings during the 1920s. Especially notable are the brilliance of the ebony spots on her numerous flaming orange poppies, and the dramatic lure of the blacks in my favorite picture *Dark Iris III* done in 1926. I first saw this as a large poster, hanging at the end of a long underground parking ramp, and was mesmerized by her vision. A dozen or so paintings—where black is used—include portrayals of morning glories, petunias, pansies, and even of the overhanging spathe of the jack-in-the-pulpit.

When contemplating the beauty in nature, we tend to think of greens and yellows and blues, of pinks and reds, of tawny beiges, rather than of black or gray which do not reflect and transmit light as the softer pastels do.

We categorize black in negative ways: the sudden descent of enveloping darkness in tropical evenings, the tossing turbulence of the storm clouds that harbor tornados within. Germany's Black Forest was so named, not because evergreen needles really were black, but because the massed trees looked black from a distance.

Many tree species have black varieties—alder, ash, cherry, gum, locust, maple, oak, walnut—apparently named from the darkness of their bark. And a black snake will slither around underneath black willows in the black dirt.

If you leaf through a wildflower guide looking for evidence of black, your stops will be few, compared to other colors. Native black-eyed Susans, favorites of the daisy family, really have chocolate-colored center disks. Black medick, a small alien prostrate clover, develops oddly-twisted black seed pods from tiny yellow flower balls. A garden escapee, blackberry lily, shows masses of black seeds in ripened pods. White baneberry, or doll's-eyes, has white seed balls with bright black spots. White-flowered black nightshade develops black berries which are totally different from the scarlet fruit of lilac-flowered nightshade. Immature berries of both vines are poisonous for humans, but safely eaten by birds of many species.

The attractive strings of button-like seeds on pokeweed appear black, but with an iridescent purple sheen. This plant is exceptional because it bears new blossoms and mature seeds simultaneously, a trait found in few flowers. The roots and possibly the berries are poisonous, but early spring shoots are widely eaten as greens. Pulp of the berries can be used for ink, giving rise to the plant's alternate name of inkberry.

Black swallowwort, an alien milkweed family vine, is presumably called black for its flowers, which are actually deep, deep purple. The ghostly, translucent, waxy, white Indian pipe—a chlorophyll-lacking saprophyte—turns black at maturity and looks strange when it stands above the snow in winter.

In the Arctic, tiny vines of black crowberry sheet the tundra rocks, bearing large crops of edible purple seeds which turn black and become tastier after a winter under the snows. Arctic rock tripe, a lichen forming on boulder surfaces, is said to be edible, but starving explorers write of being ill after eating it.

In Holland, black tulips were exceedingly stylish at one time, with sales so high that the investment market was totally upset. Alexander Dumas built his novel, *Black Tulip*, around this odd historical event.

Gills of the common light gray inky cap mushroom blacken at maturity and dissolve into pitch-black liquid.

The natural world specializes in the greens and yellows, blues and reds we all love, but if you keep sharp watch you really will find black here and there in petals and bark and especially in seeds.

November 6, 1999

Listen Carefully

IN TODAY'S FAST-MOVING WORLD, many lovely nature sounds are lost in traffic roar or buried by loud music. But when it's possible, experiencing the outdoors with our ears can be delightful.

Water, in amounts both large and small, has a vast repertoire of tones. One sleeping room in our old summer cottage boasted a corrugated tin roof. Rain dropping rhythmically was a favorite lullaby, and acorns dropping were sudden waker-uppers.

On windless days, Lake Michigan lies smooth and serene, but even then wavelets come lapping in, barely audible. When wind picks up a little, they move more rapidly and the word susurration describes perfectly the constantly repeated cadence.

On stormy days, when the lake plays at being an ocean, breakers come tumbling, crashing, and roaring in, making speech impossible but providing a wonderful opportunity to revel in uncontrollable wildness. The great volume of descending water at Niagara Falls also blocks out all communication.

The back and forth movement of tides on salt water coasts is always a matter of wonder to me. How can such enormous amounts of a substance as heavy as water move so fast, so far, so regularly, so stealthily, yet almost soundless?

Poets for centuries have written about the tinkling song of the brook, the soft little purl and swish. From Hal Borland's *Sundial of the Seasons* comes: "True, the voice of the brook is no more than the sound of water flowing downhill. Reduce it to an explanation and the song remains, . . . a voice of change, a psalm of the surgent season."

Summer campers in woodland areas enjoy sleeping under the stars to catch glimpses of the moon sailing along serenely, but veterans remember a negative factor, too. When mosquitoes are at their peaks, one who has survived that constant drone and buzz never forgets it. But lying by water's edge listening sleepily to a screech owl's shimmery call is to feel that this is the best of all possible worlds. A strident *who cooks for you* from a barred owl can be intimidating, making you shrink into your sleeping bag, but you revel in his wildness at the same time. Reveille is preceded with the constant mourning of doves and even the faraway call of a loon.

When walking brushy woodland trails, has a covey of grouse exploded almost under your feet, really startling you? One must admire their defensive technique.

Tree trunks rubbing together can make startling

noises, too, because the squeaking is hard to identify. And branches blowing in heavy wind create a deafening uproar, often tumultuous, always alarming, wildness to be enjoyed. Mother Nature still has ways we cannot control, and experiencing them is awesome.

Theories about bird song techniques and intentions have filled pages and pages for years, so comments here are limited. To hear a hummingbird beating his tiny wings is a rare privilege. It is like a small motor idling, so fast and steady, powering his maneuvers up, down, back, forward, or just standing on air.

Another privilege, totally different, a symbol of true wildness, is the bugling of sandhill cranes, calling high, high in the sky.

Skylarks, too, like to be way up there and they sing and sing and sing while hovering. What marvelous breath control they have.

One of my top ten bird songs, heard all too rarely in these days of fragmentation of our woodlands, is the lilting, flute-like voice of the wood thrush. This song never fails to stop me in my tracks. How can this small set of organs create such ethereal music? Carson often wrote of the deep joy she found in the songs of veeries and hermit thrushes when she heard them in both Maryland and Maine.

Have you walked a sandy beach when the wind swept furiously up or down the shore, when sand piled up behind each little stone, creating microscopic dunes?

The fast-moving grains seemed to lisp, even to whistle, as they sped by, excoriating and flaying our skin in passing. Later, you found the rhythmic ripple marks, the wind's autograph.

We do not cherish the annoying drone of seventeen-year locusts. However unwelcome their din, we must marvel at their secret agenda and unseen abundance. Wing-scratching katydids, sibilant cicadas, and rattly crickets make summer hours vibrate, a cheerful if monotonous din. Frost will still their voices, closing the door on another year.

In 1996, the froggers became a new group of observers in our naturalist population. Because frogs are in danger everywhere, scientists and wildlife specialists are trying to count them systematically. Volunteers go out on spring nights listening for the calls and clunks of local species and report findings to the Michigan Department of Natural Resources.

So whatever the season or the habitat, keep on the alert for new sounds more unique and less threatening than thunderclaps.

September 28, 1996

Life at 62°5' North

Refrigerator-sized chunks of ice move back and forth, back and forth, pushed by a forty-two-foot tide as the July sun breaks up Frobisher Bay's solid ice sheet three degrees, or 200 miles, south of the Arctic Circle. Multiyear ice pieces are an eerie blue. The amount of power involved in such a constantly shifting scene is truly mind-boggling.

From the shore, I see that wings and tails of passing ravens have numerous feathers missing. Numbers of them crisscross this Baffin Island valley many times a day, pausing to harass a newly fed dog and croaking hoarsely from roosting spots on roofs and power poles.

Brilliant white snow buntings whistle loudly as they float from rock to rock. Females are guarding eggs or hatchlings under a boulder nearby. Lapland longspurs whistle their *ticky-tick-tew* from rocky eminences. Sooner or later, redpolls and wheatears will appear.

But the real heroes of this barren scene of vast skies, rocky tundra, icy sea, and snow-streaked mountains are the plants which have only four weeks in which to flower and set seed. All are perennials, with grass family members dominant. Mosses and lichens abound.

As I write on July 4th, the thermometer reads fifty degrees—not an optimum temperature for plant development—yet more than a score of tiny flower species are in full blossom. Sheets of arctic white heather and mountain avens are the most apparent. Tiny pink bells on bilberry's ground-hugging branches are everywhere, mingling with Lapland lousewort and *Diapensia* hummocks. Lingonberry and bearberry are creeping fruit bearers.

Arctic labrador tea and prickly saxifrage are dwarfed, but the genera are the same ones found in Michigan. Plants can grow no higher than snow depth because of the desiccating, abrasive winter winds.

Moss campion's tiny hot pink flowers grow in dense brilliant green cushions. Like many arctic plants, campion has a flexible tap root anchoring it in spaces between rocks.

Four magenta-to-purple colored flowers are dotted here and there: alpine azalea, purple saxifrage, broadleaved willow herb, and purple mountain heather.

On the sandy beach, a few alien dandelions are in flower where animal or man has left extra nitrogen. Cushions of sandwort mingle with wormwood, a miniature version of the Great Lakes artemisia. *Mertensias* hug the sand with flattened mounds of electric blue and pink floral sprays.

In the wrack line are ten- to twelve-foot-long kelps left by high tide waters, along with bits of caribou fur, occasional gull feathers, and a variety of bones.

At edges of the tiny stream, which carries permafrost meltwater down to the bay, are stalks of alpine bistort where flowers are replaced by bulblets that sprout and fall off to grow new plants without a seed generation.

Thrift is found in dense tufts of round pink flower heads, growing on long leafless stalks. Its old plant parts linger from year to year to provide warmth.

One of the gayest plants and also the best adapted to difficult conditions is the hardy arctic poppy which grows as high up and as far north as there is any soil. Internal antifreeze enables it to freeze each night but still flower repeatedly. Cup-shaped, bright yellow blossoms follow the sun, concentrating warmth and inviting pollinating insects to share the heat. Single flowers, borne on slender arching stems which grow out of compact hairy leaf rosettes, develop into small green barrels filled with ever-so-many tiny seeds. When dry and black, the spoked barrel head develops openings just like a salt shaker.

Poppies and other species which hug the ground when in flower grow taller when flowering is finished so that the wind will spread the seed. Melting snows also help with distribution.

By the end of July, beach *Mertensia* blossoms turn into nutlets with spongy outer coats, which become inflated and therefore support dispersal by sea.

Summer weather is generally pleasant, if always windy. Temperatures stay in the upper fifties most days with sixty-eight the warmest I've experienced in six Baffin Island summers. Drizzle and rapidly shifting fogs are common. Most of the Arctic is a desert with about as much precipitation as Arizona's Sonora Desert—ten inches a year—thus, real rain as we know it is uncommon. Glaciers, icecaps, mountains, and the presence of a large body of water mean that clouds change constantly, a never-ending delight.

One evening, returning from a small plane flight over Frobisher Bay, we encountered a light rain shower. Suddenly, a full rainbow spanning the horizon appeared before us, and we flew right through the leg of the arc.

Caribous' round black droppings scattered over the tundra remind one of the large animal herd browsing on lichens, grasses, sedges, and willow twigs in the winter. In summer, the herds move inland to the edge of Baffin's icecap, away from bothersome insects.

Because the Arctic's season of frost-free days is short, it may take from several to twenty years for invertebrates to mature and complete their reproductive cycles. Therefore, I am delighted when I find a wooly bear caterpillar. Mosquitoes, houseflies, and no-see-ums are all identifiable. On bright sunny days, occasional sulphur butterflies flit over the tiny flowers. On landing, they position themselves so that their wings are tilted to receive maximum warmth from the sun's rays. Undersides of those wings are sulphur yellow, fringed with a narrow band of pink scales.

Grass, sedge, and flower seeds develop quickly, a result of long hours of sunlight. Last summer, I wandered the tundra gathering tiny black poppy seeds and scattered a plentiful supply on a rocky hillside outside the kitchen window where we are encouraging native flowers. Two families of just-fledged soft gray baby snow buntings, white wing and tail patches flashing, spent hours enjoying the unexpected bonus. Their presence was a bonus for us.

August 15 and 22, 1998

Why So White?

Have you ever puzzled over trying to identify a bird that has white feathers in unexpected places? Who has white field marks that aren't illustrated in any field guide? The lack of normal coloring, called albinism, always comes as an intriguing surprise.

Birds, other animals, or plants which are totally devoid of pigment are termed albino and those with just abnormal areas of white are albinistic. The complete albino has no pigment in skin, hair, or eyes. Eyes appear pink, because, in the absence of pigments, the blood in capillaries shows pink. We notice this in white mice, white rabbits, and white farmyard poultry. Birds that are normally white, such species as swans, gulls, or geese which have normal coloring in feet, legs, and bills aren't in this category.

Because humans with this uncommon condition have no pigment to protect the iris of the eye, they must wear dark glasses in bright light conditions.

Patches of white that you observe in a bird, often in the tail, are genetic in origin, and may have been inherited from one or both parents. Albinistic traits are most commonly found among robins, blackbirds, crows, and hawks, birds which are all or predominantly dark in color. One report indicates that as many as thirty-five percent of a flock of red-winged blackbirds may show odd colorings.

Yellow or red birds—such as goldfinches, cardinals, or orioles—are less apt to have any white feathers. Brown pigment seems to be the color most likely to disappear.

Terres, in *The Audubon Encyclopedia of North American Birds*, reports some degree of albinism in 304 species. Robins had about eight percent of the records, leading all others. House sparrows followed with about five and one half percent of 1,047 cases of albinism reported by one author; only seven percent were total or complete albinos.

An American robin with pink eyes was caught by a cat in Amsterdam, New York, and lived as a pet for five years. Melanistic robins, with all dark or black pigmentation, also were reported. In the spring of 1953 near Dearborn, Michigan, three young robins were flying with a normal parent; one youngster was pure white and two were gray.

The gene for albinism is recessive; both parents must carry it for it to appear in offspring in either albino or albinistic conditions.

A brood of four all-white blue jays was sighted in

Illinois. In hummingbirds, individuals with all-white feathers are frequently reported, but the eyes have usually been dark.

Unfortunately, the slightly different individual is often treated as an outcast by other birds. When a completely white female red-winged blackbird was harassed mercilessly by flock members, she always returned to the flock. An albinistic barn swallow experienced nothing but chasing by other members of the flock.

In all human races, complete albinos occur in about one in 20,000. Higher incidences occur in the Caribbean among the San Blas Indians. In the case of marriage of two albinos, records indicate that all children are affected.

Reference books show pictures of albino squirrels and salamanders, indicating that this abnormality can occur throughout the animal kingdom. One family made a pet of a captive pink-eyed flying squirrel.

August 12, 1995

Now You See It...

MOTHER NATURE'S BAG OF WONDERS sometimes seems bottomless. Can one ever understand all of the mechanisms? Camouflage, for instance.

In the natural world the polar bear, top carnivore of the north, matches his surroundings, remaining white year round because he lives in a land of perpetual ice and snow. The female even dens in a snowbank, giving birth to pure white young. The white pelage serves the bears well when they creep along in pursuit of an unwary seal or an arctic hare, whose coat is white in winter only.

Two other arctic species, the fox and the ptarmigan, both pure white in winter, hunt on the tundra in short northern summers, when their fur and feathers slowly change to mottled brown shades, shifting back to white again when days grow shorter and the long, cold arctic night moves in.

Snowy owls and some of the magnificent arctic gyrfalcons are largely white to help in their hunting. The hardy ivory gull—who never leaves ice and snow—is a lovely white all year with only its legs and bill colored black.

In southwest Michigan, the long-tailed weasel, who does not hibernate, changes its fur from brown to white in winter, as protection against predators. Its tail is always black, as is that of the ptarmigan. Scientists think that melanistic pigments help reduce excessive wear.

In tropical regions, the giraffe, the zebra, the leopard, and the tiger all have spots or stripes because they live in forests where sun's rays peaking through trees create a dappled effect. The spotty appearance helps animals to be less conspicuous.

Gray tree frogs "can be gray, green, or brown, and can change between various shades of these colors," says the Michigan State University's *Field Guide to Toads, Frogs, and Salamanders*. What a fine, flexible protective palette it has.

Even our little crab spider can change his color enabling him to disappear into the background. Resting on a white flower, its coloring is white, but changes to yellow on a yellow flower.

A box turtle, one of the longest-lived turtles, has a mottled black and yellow back that helps it to be inconspicuous in its wanderings through the forest. Because it lives to such a great age, maybe the coloring does protect it—in addition to an ingenious hinge arrangement, which enables it to shut its top shell, the carapace, and bottom shell, the plastron, together tightly.

Feather colors in some of our nesting bird species suggest camouflage as a help in protective concealment. The subdued plumage of many female birds may protect them in their long, quiet hours incubating eggs and brooding young.

A scarlet tanager breeding male is an extreme example of brilliant coloring, the red emphasized by the contrasting black wings, tail, and bright black eye. In the fall, however, he is amazingly blotched with red, yellow, and green, like autumn foliage. Finally, all the red disappears and he is left with a green back and yellow underparts, much like his mate's cryptic year-round plumage.

Black bands across the killdeer's breast break up its outline, rendering it less visible.

Mimicry is another protective device for avoiding hungry predators. A walking stick does indeed resemble a stick and is often overlooked. The shape and coloring of the praying mantis render it almost invisible, too, as it mimics the shape and coloring of the plants it rests on. Some caterpillars resemble bird droppings.

Finally, the viceroy butterfly escapes its enemies by being colored to resemble a monarch butterfly, whose body contains unpleasant tasting acids which hungry birds learned to avoid long ago.

July 1, 1995

Snowbound in November

As I write, before noon, Tuesday, November 12th, the governing word of our lives is spelled W-H-I-T-E as snow flakes keep falling and falling, and falling some more, hour after hour. Widely separated, they seem to come almost straight down because winds, blessedly, are not active today. Facing north, one feels a slight draft, but leaves are motionless.

On this, the fourth day of our surprise lake effect storm, the weather channel still is carrying a ninety percent prediction of snow for tomorrow. City people everywhere are inconvenienced, many seriously, by this freak avalanche of soft stuff, but if you have time and temperament to walk outside just for pleasure, joys are at every hand. Stop by a woods on a snowy morn!

Soft wet flakes falling on my sleeve collapse almost on contact. I can see that most of them are not single crystals, but rather delicate aggregations of four or five, clinging together. Looking closely, I can distinguish a few exquisite six-pointed stars. Such a magnificence of minute beauty is rarely available and calls for finding a magnifying glass.

More than 400 years ago, Swedish archbishop Olaus Magnum, blessed with a heaven-sent curiosity bump, prepared a woodcut portraying the nature of snow crystals. But the real hero of such study is Wilson "Snowflake" Bentley, a doughty Vermonter, who made the world's first photomicrograph of such a crystal in 1885. Working for more than forty years, usually in below freezing cold, he captured some 4,500 different snow crystals on film with the most primitive homemade camera apparatus. The Dover reprint of his *Snow Crystals* is well worth your study—a mind-boggling array of nature's extravagance, its delicate and intricate charms. Another delightful book, if you want to pursue crystal study, is *Field Guide to Snow Crystals* by Edward R. LaChapelle.

Most trees in the nearby snow-filled woodlands are bare now, with white birches a notable exception. The yellowed leaves turn them into torches in an otherwise whitened landscape. Some of their remaining inch-long male catkins are neatly frosted.

The needles on spruces and cedars are short and arranged close together, providing excellent repositories for accumulation of large masses of snow. It is behind these puffy pillows that our small winter resident song birds huddle awaiting better foraging conditions. Fortunately, most of our winged migrants have moved on south and have not been caught by this prolonged, unseasonal storm.

Because the air is so still, some of the dangling seed balls on sycamore trees even have crystal tiaras. Bright scarlet and orange berries on nightshade vines are gay as can be, set off by clusters of white flakes where vine stems and tendrils are thick. Such a contrast gives one camera itch.

People who live forty to fifty miles east of Lake Michigan are often spared negative lake effect weather. This time, the vast mass of frigid arctic air sent by Canada picked up such a supersaturated overload of moisture, from the as yet warm lake, that the sky just keeps on dumping and dumping that water in the form of snow.

The air is clear save for drifting flakes, no fog, no mist. Clouds are predominantly light toned in color with only a few in gradations of gray. As they slowly shift, a veiled but luminous sun occasionally glows through the pale overcast. Despite the absence of real sunlight, the world is incredibly light because every surface has been whitewashed. Were the sun to break through, the glare would be so glorious as to be blinding. Our world is as pure today as if we were in the Arctic.

This early in the winter season, food is plentiful for foraging birds and other animals, but I saw no evidence of wildlife movement this morning. Rabbits and squirrels must be holed up. No sound, no motion—just vivid awareness of this expanse of beauty, this calm and peace. No caw of crow, no honk of goose broke the snow-in-sulated silence.

Closely spaced buds on forsythia bushes trapped mounds of white in their branches. Long-stemmed rose hip clusters on the multiflora bushes have shaken off snowy coats, but their thickly interlaced branches are filled with fluffy white foam.

A few twisted yellow petals on the witch-hazel tree are tipped with snow, and most petals are hanging a little limp at twenty-three degrees. In the vegetable garden, I harvested little sprigs of broccoli four days ago and now each plant has a perfectly shaped dome resembling a giant vanilla ice cream cone. Abandoned bird nests, now exposed, have similar domes.

In a sheltered corner, limp Japanese maple leaves are bravely yellow and scarlet—all well-frosted. Shiny green leaves on the pear trees have retained some scarlet too; they would make lovely patterns for a kaleidoscope.

This early storm is an unexpected bonanza for snowman makers and skiers, too, but what a run store-keepers must have had on their winter boot and snow shovel supplies.

Maybe it's a good day to stay inside and read John Greenleaf Whittier's poem, *Snowbound*.

November 23, 1996

Winter Survival

The Calvin and Hobbes comic strip that Bill Watterson drew for so long was always a favorite of mine and I was saddened when he gave it up. In the last column, the conversation which took place between the two characters is worth repeating:

> Calvin: *Wow! It really snowed last night. Isn't it wonderful?*
> Hobbes: *Everything familiar has disappeared. The world looks brand-new.*
> C. *A New Year... A fresh clean start.*
> H. *It's like having a big white sheet of paper to draw on.*
> C. *A day full of possibilities... It's a magical world, Hobbes ol' Buddy... Let's go exploring!*

Such an invitation is always welcome to nature lovers. Where to go today? But, in winter, exploring takes extra effort to collect comfortable protective clothing and gear, fill the thermos, clear snow and ice from steps and car, etc. But still, how much better equipped we are to deal with this season than are other living things.

The north wind doth blow
And we shall have snow
And what will the robin do then?
Poor thing!

Days of intense cold, wild wind, and persistent snow create conditions of severe hardship for creatures of the natural world. Each species has developed clever individual ways of coping, of surviving, or else it wouldn't be here. The fittest have survived again.

The shortness of days reduces feeding hours significantly and is a major factor in birds' lives. We may have nine hours of daylight now, but as many as sixteen in June. Chickadees, nuthatches, titmice, and downy woodpeckers must be active every minute to find enough to eat. They troop the woods together on the principle that many eyes see more than just a few eyes. It's unusual for birds to feed in mixed flocks, but this group has learned that energy conservation is the key to winter survival.

A Wisconsin bird bander and wild life ecologist, who conducted an elaborate chickadee survival study, found that in mild winter weather a black-capped chickadee needs 150 sunflower seeds a day, but at zero degrees needs 250 of them. The latter figure represents sixty percent of his body weight. Imagine that you had to find food equaling sixty percent of your body weight every day. But such desperate need helps explain the ping-pong-like activity of a chickadee as he bounces from feeder to branch and back. No wimp, he.

Teale wrote that ultrahigh speed films reveal that chickadee wings beat about thirty times a second, about three-fourths of the speed of a hummingbird. Chicky can alter course in 3/100s of a second. After exercise, that little heart may beat one thousand times a minute, while even at rest it goes at 500. At night, the bird goes dormant to conserve energy, lowering their usual 112 degrees some eighteen or twenty degrees, producing deep torpor but saving energy.

At night, bluebirds, nuthatches, and winter wrens seek out nest boxes or tree holes and roost with others of their own species, sharing heat and shutting out cold.

Some years, we have invasions of flocks of common redpolls as winter drags on and the north country becomes more and more inhospitable. They, like chickadees, are in constant motion, with their movements creating warmth, but also consuming energy, requiring more food intake. In the low Arctic, redpolls dance from birch tree to birch tree, picking off a mouthful of tiny seeds in passing.

Redpolls have a unique little pouch on the side of the esophagus. If they can fill it with seed before bedtime, their digestion proceeding all night keeps them from freezing.

Some birds grow more feathers in winter, the same way we use layers of clothing. Goldfinches may add as many as one thousand. Although lifeless, feathers are tightly constructed and are excellent conservers of heat. In order to create insulating air pockets, birds can tense tiny muscles in their skin, turning their bodies into fluff balls.

Deer hair is hollow, and the air-filled tubes provide excellent insulation. Snowflakes do not melt when they fall on their hides. Prolonged deep snow, preventing them from moving around, is their worst enemy. They can survive cold but must have adequate food.

Squirrels and foxes use their long furry, flexible tails as blankets, and stay quiet awaiting favorable weather before resuming activity. Some chipmunks will hibernate, but others emerge for feeding at irregular times.

Most woodchucks and thirteen-lined ground squirrels go into true hibernation from late October to March, thus surviving by avoiding winter. But they must have completed a successful fall feeding binge to provide necessary nourishing layers of fat.

Snowshoe hares in the far north grow fur on the soles of their feet, making handy mukluks.

Many rabbits enjoy snow because it gives them a higher feeding platform and access to additional supplies. We learned this with sorrow, several years ago, when prolonged heavy snows were followed by freezing sleet and bitter cold. The rabbits ate every single bit of thirty tasty Iowa crab saplings that reached above their twenty-four-inch protective plastic tubing. The trees survived, and this year a few flowered, but at the time my grief and frustration at the loss were immeasurable!

Horses, like humans, need exercise to keep in good trim, but icy conditions are dangerous for them. A fall and a broken leg are usually fatal.

Sleet storms are a threat to quail, wild turkeys, and grouse because their tails may freeze to the ground. Each autumn, grouse grow a sort of snowshoe, an extra tissue edge to toes, which helps them travel in deep snow. Pheasants, nonnative birds, have no such adaptation and are extremely vulnerable to ice storms or deep snow.

In zero weather, ground-feeding birds will alternate feet, pulling first one and then the other into body feathers. Or they will sink down over both feet. Ravens feeding in snow keep up a unique nonstop jumping motion, perhaps to keep from freezing to the ground.

In *Secret Language of Snow*, Terry Tempest Williams wrote that the Inuit, who live in snow most of their lives, have many descriptive words for it. Falling snow is Annui, on the ground it is Api, that which swirls like smoke is Sequiq, and snow collected in trees is Qali. Do you think birds and other animals know the difference?

February 2, 1997

255

That Dratted White Stuff

WHAT'S THE LARGEST AMOUNT OF SNOW ever recorded in the United States during one twenty-four-hour period? Forty inches? Fifty? Sixty? No—more. Seventy-six inches fell on Silver Lake near Boulder, Colorado, in 1921. How could you cope with that much snow? It's hard to even imagine. Losses of wildlife species must have been disastrous.

Where do they come from—these fragile hexagons that can so upset our plans? Our automobile-dependent culture shorts out when we have to work our way out of more than ten or twelve inches of white stuff.

Southwest Michigan is noted for lake effect snow storms which delight poets, photographers, and artists but may punish the rest of us. Such storms occur when arctic winds blow across the vast expanse of the yet warm Lake Michigan, picking up moisture as they go. When they blow over cooler land, the snow load is suddenly dumped. Northwest Indiana, Michigan's west shore, Cleveland, and Buffalo are all too familiar with the lake effect phenomenon.

Sometimes the snow is dry, granular, and accompanied by harsh northwest winds of twenty to thirty mph causing significant blowing and drifting, making plowing north-south roads an exercise in futility. If heavy snow and sustained winds of at least thirty-five mph are accompanied by low temperatures, the meteorologists call the storm a blizzard and say, "Stay home". Blizzard snow is fine and powdery, particles that sting and blind dangerously. Whiteouts are frequent.

The first ten days of January 1999 brought us a blizzard, then hours and hours of zero cold and heavy flurries. The total snowfall brought us nearly two-thirds of the expected year's total of sixty-five inches. There were also many hours of significant wind chill, a figure which combines the joint effect of wind and temperature, useful in helping us plan needed protection. A twenty mph wind at zero degrees yields a wind chill rating of minus thirty-nine degrees, compared to what it would be without the wind.

What causes this white stuff, these fragile hexagons that make our world appear so delectable? On January 10th, after thirty inches of snow had fallen here, we figured that a friend with 185 acres of land owned about 20,146,500 cubic feet of snow—an incredible volume.

Ice storms are unwonted phenomena, but all too well-known. Our October 28th, 1997, ice storm caused millions of dollars of damage to vegetation and utility facilities. Dead trees and branches went down as usual, but limbs from living trees still holding their leaves broke off from the weight of ice on the leaves, deforming many beautiful old shade trees. It was weeks before all the debris was cleared up.

Why review all these sad, expensive traumas that help car dealers and landscaping services, but put the rest of us in despair? They serve to remind us that our mechanized, automated, computerized civilization can still be brought to its knees by nature's whim. When power goes out and roads are impassable, we're pretty helpless.

The components of a snowflake are invisible to us. A bit of dust meets a bit of moisture far away in a cloud, and a snowflake is born. After that, everything depends on the moisture, temperature, and winds the flake meets as it falls. A full-grown snowflake may change its shape a dozen times before it reaches us.

Meteorologists tell of various forms of snow crystals: plate, hexagon, cylinder, and needle. We've all been taught that every snowflake is different from every other one, despite the millions that fall. Hexagonal symmetry—familiar to us since grade-school days—can readily be seen if you have a hand lens and a dark coat sleeve, but also watch for other forms. Days of fluffy sticky flakes bring the prettiest ones if you can stop breathing long enough to study them. In addition to snow flakes themselves, there are many permutations: freezing rain, graupel, sleet, hoar frost, rime, icicles—even glaciers—and each a wondrous form in itself. One October day, we were walking a favorite trail and experienced two short periods of an unusual kind of precipitation. We were deluged with tiny striated perfect ice cones, about one-third of an inch tall. We called it hail, for lack of a better name. They were noisy as they fell on the trail's dry leaves and all appeared to be identical.

There are still those of us who, properly dressed for punishing arctic blasts and deep drifts, enjoy prowling a glittery or snow-iced woods on a blue sky day. We return, exhausted, exhilarated, and stimulated by the constant floundering and the beauty of elongated blue shadows cast by the low-lying winter sun. Such trips bring to mind visions of *Over the River and Through the Woods* or even a Russian troika.

December 25, 1999

259

Winter Woodland Colors

WINTER WOODLAND WALKS can often seem dull and monotonous, but the bright-eyed and questing observer can always find a few, albeit small, colorful items to enjoy.

We take the dun, drab, brown of oak trunk bark for granted, but they say if you look at it with your head held upside down you'll discover blue and maroon shades you never suspected.

Studying evergreen needles, observers find subtle shadings varying from the dull grayish-green of junipers to the light blue-green of white pines. Look closely at a white pine needle to find the fine blue line on the upper surface, lines so plentiful they must affect the tree's overall appearance. Delicate concentric circles of lichens ornament many tree trunks with fine chartreuse designs.

Purplish-blue berries on red cedars, also called junipers, are covered with a glaucous powdery bloom and appear in abundance every two or three years. The frequency of cedars along Michigan highways speaks to the way in which hungry birds help to reproduce this reddish and raggedy-barked tree.

In moist wooded areas, evergreen ferns are visible even after heavy snows. Christmas ferns on shaded hillsides are the richest, most insistent green. Wood fern flaunts tall, broad fronds in damp woods. Sensitive fern leaves are long gone, as their name implies, but their odd fertile stalks, resembling little brown beads on a string, persist even into the second year. Among them, watch for areas of evergreen club mosses. Ground pine is a handsome, low-growing ally, protected in Michigan.

Scarlet berries on Japanese barberry and Michigan holly, and clusters of fruit on hawthorn trees, add a pleasant accent. These foods sustain over-wintering bright-breasted robins and demurely clad hermit thrushes. At edges of wet woods, there may still be a few tiny red globes on partridge berry vines, which persists through the winter unless ruffed grouse, wild turkeys, or white-footed mice find them.

Juicy red fruits dangling from high-bush cranberry, a wetland-loving *Viburnum*, will lure burnished gold cedar waxwings.

On a crisp, cold, sunny day, keep your eye on the sky, watching for sundogs, bright, rainbow-colored bits of sun's reflections on ice crystals in high cirrostratus clouds. Parhelia, as scientists call these ephemera, are rarer than rainbows and disappear quickly as the angle of the sun changes. Arctic areas have many fascinating variations on tinted arcs and ice-cloud halos in relation to sun and moon, ice crystals, and water droplets. Like the reputed green flash at sunset, the physics of refraction, reflection, and diffraction are beyond my comprehension, but the eerie phenomena are wonderful to experience. If you're fortunate enough to spot a sundog, try to record its elapsed time and figure out its degree of altitude.

Similarly, dazzling sunlight reflections on icicles and glittering ice-sheeted trees add varied colors to winter woods. Sleet and ice storms create every shade of the spectrum when the sun emerges, making memorable, crystalline rainbow effects wherever you look.

Gray birch trunks tend to appear washed out, accented with large, black triangular patches below each branch, whereas white or paper birches make a distinctive bright white accent, visible through the woods for some distance.

Remaining leaves on gray dogwood bushes are a warm maroon and their empty, leftover fruit stems remain scarlet all winter. Tiny, round bud globes on linden trees are also scarlet, as are the late-ripening hips on swamp rose bushes.

Pokeweed stems stay magenta long after raccoons and migrating thrushes have devoured their strings of unique button-like seeds.

Last year's hepatica leaves hold their liverish color through the snows, a great help in locating the plants in March when the woodsman's heart longs for sight of their protective fuzz around hidden new leaves.

Autumn olive leaves often cling to branches through December and January. Brisk winds make their silvery undersides visible. Shoulder-high maple-leaved viburnum shrubs hold festoons of blue-black berries in shaded woodlands. Because of their low fat content, these seeds are eaten only as a last resort.

On a bright winter day, after a period of severe winter weather, a flash of reddish-brown fur says that red squirrels are feeding again. Squirrels, chipmunks, and raccoons tend to hole up for long periods until a combination of moderating temperature and extreme hunger lures them from nests, adding rich new shades of rust and russet to somber winter landscapes.

The emergence of snow fleas at their late winter mating time creates a lively black and white scene. These tiny springtails live in the debris around tree bases, eating dead material there. Suddenly, snow comes alive with thousands and thousands of them as their pogostick tails send them bouncing along. If you could jump to the same proportion as the pencil-point sized *Collembola*, you could jump over a twelve-story building.

Silvery-gray beeches flaunt gauzy bleached leaves all winter, and nearby bronzy box elder seeds dance in large clusters. In swamps, cattail leaves have faded to parchment tones, but one author says their fruiting stalks are "ruddy exclamation points" amid dangling blackish-brown alder cones.

Watercress and duckweed in creeks and ponds stay green, even under ice. They must have a never-ending source of antifreeze in their veins.

Leaden wind-filled clouds of winter match the back of the dark-eyed junco as he vigorously digs away snow around Queen Anne's lace and black-eyed Susans, scrambling for sustenance in a not too friendly all-white world.

Purplish shades of shadows on the snow and amethyst surfaces of blackberry canes are subtle colors, but brilliant low anchored clouds of winter sunsets can offer much joy for winter-weary woods walkers seeking relief from a white monotony.

January 10, 1998

Make a Thinkpiece

Michigan's artist-naturalist Gwen Frostic has a charming little booklet, *To Those Who See*, dedicated to those "with wonder in their hearts". Ever so many folk— through indifference or lack of knowledge—walk woodland paths unaware of the interesting things they're passing.

One of my favorite seeing-eye activities—for over half a century—has been collecting objets d'nature to be converted into objets d'art, usually into wreaths. All it takes is awareness of nature's gifts, time and places to roam, ample pockets and, later, cardboard and Elmer's Glue-All.

A wreath of dried objects will be just as attractive as the quality and variety of items collected. I've been exercising my pack rat instinct for many years, and title the assemblages thinkpieces. I cut eight-inch discs from heavy cardboard cartons, remove a three-inch central circle, leaving a wreath shape about two to three inches wide. I then attach a hanging wire, with ends tucked inside where they'll be covered by cones or whatever.

Don't try to place too many items at one sitting. I find it practical to have three or four wreaths going at once. Place major emphasis pieces, larger cones or seeds or shells, in position at first. When the glue is firm, fill in around them with smaller objects, acorns or small cones, always keeping proportion, color relationships, and overall design in mind. What will be the focal point? Are some items you've saved, like sweet gum balls, too large? Can they be cut in half?

The Christmas wreath I hung on my door in 1998, dated 1984 on the back, contains outdoor souvenirs from Arizona, Florida, and California, as well as from around the Great Lakes. Now that I wander Baffin Island arctic tundra in summers, I don't find sea shells or good seeds, but leftovers from dog feeding—caribou and seal teeth—add interest.

Limit proportions of white materials, for accent only, lest they seem out of place with dominant beiges and browns. Pine cones of all kinds and sizes are basic, and can even be used alone, but I like mixtures better than just one variety. Leathery European larch cones keep their shape for years and add a pleasing repetitious note. Alder cones often grow in groups of twos and threes and make interesting accents. Small cones from casuarina, hemlock, and tamarack trees are useful. White cedar cones are flimsy but, if picked green enough, add useful pattern.

Oriental and Shirley poppy seeds, tiny gourds,

mock-orange seeds, even columbine seed vases, work up well. Beechnut husks, acorns of all kinds and sizes, cotton bolls, peach and plum pits, pecans, Brazil nuts, shagbark hickory nuts, gnawed black walnut halves— all can be fitted in, lending color and line interest.

Slippery, flat seeds from wisteria pods, and dried turkey tail fungus pieces cover exposed edges nicely, as do small angel wing and coquina shells; even pumpkin seeds are good edgers. If you know where a sycamore grows, peel off the fluffy seeds and use the seed's hard center core, covered with fine net. Spiral lines on shells of land snails add an interesting pattern. Chestnut burs are strong accents, but are murder on your fingers.

Texture components are harder to find because of their fragility. Bits of goldenrod or pearly everlasting may do. Sensitive fern spore stalks, whose spore sacs have not opened, are useful. Chambered fruits of velvet leaf, with their circular symmetry, can be used whole or in sections. Silver-gray immature milkweed pods have a downy surface. Sections of paper wasp's hexagonally-arranged nests are interesting but, like white materials, have to be used sparingly to keep the beige-brown tone dominant. If squirrels leave any hazelnuts, those clusters are attractive.

Cone slices, made with strong pruning shears, and smaller jack and Scotch pine cones can serve as both major accent and filler. Fill in the wreath solidly by wrapping smaller objects in groups of twos and threes in four-inch square sections of old nylons. No cardboard should show when you're finished.

Some folks add seasonal ribbons, touches of gold paint, or bright decor items, but I like the perfection of the natural objects to remain unadulterated.

Spray colorless acrylic plastic lightly over the entire surface. You can renew it as years pass. Remember that Elmer's Glue is water soluble, so these wreaths are for indoor use only.

November 27, 1999

Inland Lakes in Winter

Slowly, slowly, as early sunbeams creep through dark trunks, feathery fog cushions shift above the frozen lake. Wintry white of earth and sky are slowly differentiated as a new day begins.

By mid-February, most inland lakes are frozen, able to sustain skaters, hockey players, curious dogs, and fishermen's huts. One could spend days monitoring changing shadows, movement of cloud forms, windblown puffs of snow, and subtle winter low light effects.

Limnologists—scientists who study fresh water—report that winter temperatures and diminished light conditions, especially under snow-covered ice, keep algae productivity low. When no photosynthesis occurs in such darkness, decomposition sets in reducing oxygen to disastrously low levels. Fish cannot survive and extensive winter kills occur, more often in shallow lakes rich in dissolved nutrients, where organic pollution from sewage, fertilizer runoff, phosphate detergents, and pesticides has occurred. Ice fishermen naturally dread such dieoffs.

Glacial activity more than 10,000 years ago led to the creation of most Michigan lakes. So-called kettle lakes formed when retreating glaciers left large blocks of ice in drifts of debris.

Even in winter's snowbanks and frozen shores, curiosity about our natural world can be turned on. Find an icy lake edge where freezing and thawing have alternated repeatedly and hunt for hidden, elegant ice structures, often resembling goblets. Search out driftwood pieces, and rolls of chara stranded on the beach. Investigate fish and bird carcasses, more savory when frozen than otherwise. Lake margins often have "cattail ranks in stiff attention," as Borland wrote in one of his sensitive nature essays.

February is a good month to have a cattail fight using the fluff instead of snow as ammunition. Your enemy may collapse from laughter long before being either smothered or defeated.

Eastman, in *The Book of Swamp and Bog*, stated:

A quick experiment, one that Thoreau delighted to perform, demonstrates how tightly the dry seeds are packed in the spike. Pull out a small tuft and watch it immediately expand to fill your hand with a downy mass.

A remarkable feature of these plants is the cattail moth caterpillar which uses the fat brown sausage-like seed heads for its winter home, surviving on the minute seeds. Chickadees, in their turn, are known to feed on the caterpillars, finding the seeds too small to be worth the trouble. Eastman has found corn grains secreted in cattail seeds, probably by blue jays looking for a handy, dry pantry.

Nature explorers can look for last year's nests among the plants, nests made by marsh wrens, swamp sparrows, or red-winged blackbirds. Keep your eyes peeled for muskrat lodges, hidden in summer.

Where ice-defying brooks that never freeze enter small lakes, tangles of emergent plants, sedges, water-willow, and reeds may join the cattails. Mallards often linger there, somehow surviving through frigid winter temperatures. One of the plants sustaining them may be the still-green duckweed, often occurring in large mats. Duckweed is reputed to be the smallest plant with the largest range of any plant in the world. Our variety, *Lemna minor*, consists simply of a tiny flat body (a thallus) with a single rootlet, that floats on the water's surface.

In swampy edge areas, skunk cabbage's green horns—which poked through the mud in August—are now stretching taller through the ice. My personal winter calendar says put on your boots and search for their flowers by Washington's birthday. Look to see if those strange inner spadices are being pollinated by flesh flies. It's truly amazing that many Arum family plants generate heat from rhizomes that may be centuries old. Eighth wonder of the world? Maybe not, but certainly amazing.

271

On February nights, lamps may appear on moonlit lakes as ice fishermen ply their trade. Winter moons "ride in cool splendor," to quote Borland. Few essayists have done as much sensitive observing and as much delightful writing as he did in his lifetime.

Mating calls, too, are parts of late winter nights. Great horned owls are already on their nests, and barred and screech owls will be before long.

Evidence of winged predators' hunting efforts can be seen in the snow where wingprints tell that a venturing hungry mouse met his demise. Such prints, especially from a large owl, are often beautifully symmetrical.

It may be too cold for stone skipping and beachcombing, but alert walkers can find many other interesting wonders to study in a cold February landscape.

February 20 and 27, 1999

Looking Back—and Ahead

As ANOTHER YEAR DRAWS to its inevitable close, our minds are filled with memories to be reenjoyed as well as with anticipation of cheerful prospects ahead.

Looking back, this rambler remembers the great blue heron making its slow and ponderous departure from a half-frozen swamp, every joint articulating, the air resonating with his hoarse cracking *frawnk*, a sound reminiscent of dinosaur days.

Many folks may remember mixed feelings of elation, awe, and fear when a magnificent, yet terrifying, winter storm swept in from Lake Michigan, grounding everyone, turning woodlands into crystal palaces. When the snow stopped falling, sunlight turned ice crystals in whitened fields into shimmering fairylands. Each puff of wind sent showers of snow flying from frosted tree branches.

Then there was the day the forest floor came alive again with the new spring, when the Nature Center's beech woods thrilled us with masses of delicate spring-beauty, hepatica, anemone, long-spurred violet, and a hillside of charming blue-eyed Mary. The woodland rang with calls of towhees and red-bellied woodpeckers. At night, a barred owl hooted by the river.

Other days, we remember pulling bags and bags of garlic mustard plants, a recent invasive alien that aims to cover all of Michigan all by itself. An Environmental Defense Fund study showed that forty-six percent of our native wildflowers are suffering from too many exotic species such as this *Alliaria petiolata*. Other monocultural alien plants that destroy ecological integrity of natural habitats—such as Amur honeysuckle—prevent forest regeneration, eliminating both woody and nonwoody native plants and the animals dependent on them

Reading and rereading my favorite natural history authors—Henry Beston, Rachel Carson, John Eastman, Hal Borland, John Madson, Ann Zwinger, and on and on through my book shelves—filled many an hour, deepened my appreciations, and sent me out in inquisitive attitude, ready to enjoy and learn more.

Summer brought weeks near the Arctic Circle, mesmerized by that incredible forty-two-foot tide, creeping in and out of the head of Frobisher Bay, a movement with a strange grandeur all its own. I relished the entire life cycle of tiny tundra plants which must bud, flower, and set seed in four short weeks in July, squeezed between the last ice of June and the first sleet storms of August.

I remember fog masses creeping in and out of California's coastal valleys as we watched from higher on the mountain, the fluffiness moving on Sandburg's little cat feet.

Mourning the loss of a friend dear to me for twenty years, I often sought solace in finding some new wonder in woods or water, some natural phenomenon, an insect gall or unique seed that we might have explored together in happy times past.

Did you see Jim Brandenburg's "North Woods Journal" in the November 1997 *National Geographic* which featured some of the ninety only-one-exposure-a-day photographs he made between an autumnal equinox and winter solstice? What would you include in your own ninety shots of autumn? I would have to select one bare tree trunk to symbolize that magic cold night in November when the leaves on ginkgo trees suddenly turned gold and blanketed the ground, creating a treasure trove of crinkly aureate leaves fine for crunchy scuffling.

What are your natural world hopes and challenges for the new year? What do you want to experience? To learn? How will you escape the daily musts? What are your three wishes for ways to replenish and renew your inner person?

Maybe you can find a copy of *Flora of Kalamazoo County, Michigan,* and check it for some sites for native plants. That book, fourteen years in the making, was started as an antidote to Depression blues of the 1930s.

Even if you're a commuter glued to a steering wheel for hours on end, you can take up cloud study or learn to identify trees along your way by their shape or think about the life style of the pheasant in the field or the V of geese overhead. Can you name five native Michigan trees? Or ten?

If you're housebound, a well-stocked variety of feeders will bring you endless hours of pleasure. Relish the bravado of the blue jay. Do a feeder count for an Audubon society. Read some Mary Oliver poetry and get goosebumps for the reality, the vitality of her descriptions. She's overfond of snakes for my taste, but each to his/her own.

What are you doing to help the next generation learn to enjoy our birds, trees, and flowers? How are you helping heighten their appreciations, insure lifelong joys? Providing automated toys or sharing a new field guide? Try the *Peterson First Guides*—they're really good.

If you find a butterfly stuck to the windshield of your car, you and your child can look at its wondrous wing pattern under magnification.

One of your parks may have specimens of all the common oaks. Identifying them is a challenge!

In May, find sanctuary in woodland fern dells or watch the mysterious orderly unfolding of tulip tree leaves. Study daily light as the sun advances. A greeny-gold twilight will delight you even if you're not Monet.

Minute-to-minute, hour-to-hour, day-to-day shifts in sunlight and shadow are fascinating to experience.

Take a leaf from vermiculturist Mary Appelhof's book and learn about earthworms and the useful manner in which they turn garbage into grade A compost.

Find patterns to enjoy: ripple marks of wave-edge deposits on a beach; gossamer tissue in the web of every leaf; Fibonacci spirals in a snail shell; the homely simplicity of field daisy and black-eyed Susan.

Get away from downtown light at night and enjoy the Milky Way or the thinnest arc of the newest moon, barely visible in violet dusk.

Can you find a bit of wilderness somewhere? Explore a site with no hand-of-man things in sight, perhaps where *A River Runs Through It.* Such a change of pace refreshes jaded spirits. Hunt out a vernal pond where Mrs. Toad, under water, is laying her string of eggs with her mate faithfully fertilizing each one as it appears.

Find your refuge; dream your dreams on a hillside blued with lupine. In November, watch for a golden tamarack torch which lights up a swamp against a leaden pearl gray sky. Enjoy the patter of rain on a tent roof and inhale a camp fire's wood smoke scent so that nature becomes real and alive.

Relive your happiest nature moments and resolve to fill the new year to overflowing with them. Ravine and ridge, dune and swale, field and forest, river and stream are out there awaiting your open mind and heart.

December 27, 1997

Acknowledgements

THE TWO INSTIGATORS of this publication are tied for first place in my list of people to thank: Valerie Noble and Monica Ann Evans, who, combining their accumulated experience, have with boundless initiative, voluntarily and double-handedly carried out the tedious footwork and headwork involved in making a book. The hours involved are as countless as stars in the sky.

Lois and Jim Richmond's delightful lakeside setting and their warm hospitality afford me woodland and wetland to rove, and seclusion to read and write. Flashing wings just out the study window are part of their Nature's Acres welcoming charms.

I am grateful to H. Lewis Batts, Jr., and Mary and Edwin Meader, who gave particularly generous support.

As always, fellow travelers on woodsy paths are a source of encouragement, challenge, and friendship. The Kalamazoo Nature Center Publication Fund has helped support the project. Kalamazoo Nature Center staff members and the Kalamazoo *Gazette* merit my warmest thanks.

The works of nature writers as varied as Ann Zwinger, Mary Oliver, and Hal Borland continue to be an inspiration. Scholars and trailmates, Richard Brewer and Elwood Ehrle have widened my interests and enriched my understanding.

Participation in conservation activity undergirds any naturalist's thinking and writing. The growing strengths of the Southwest Michigan Land Conservancy give ample opportunity for prowling new wild acres and for stewardship tasks on their many preserves. Local chapters of the Audubon Society and the Michigan Botanical Club provide rich outdoor learning experiences.

For the second time, I enjoyed working with illustrator Elizabeth Henderson. She has the knack for turning what I see and write about into visual interpretations.

Once again, I appreciate Ann Paulson's design and technical know-how. Her cheerful optimism was always encouraging.

Emma Pitcher

Common and Scientific Names
Alien species are marked with an *

A
Adder's tongue. *See* Lily, trout
Alder
  black. *See* Holly, Michigan
  speckled, *Alnus rugosa*
Alpine
  azalea, *Loiseleuria procumbens*
  bistort, *Polygonum viviparum*
American
  crab, *Pyrus coronaria*
  crow, *Corvus brachyrhyncos*
  elm, *Ulmus americanus*
  goldfinch, *Carduelis tristis*
  hazelnut, *Corylus americana*
  kestrel, *Falco sparverius*
  linden. *See* Basswood
  redstart, *Setophaga ruticilla*
  robin, *Turdus migratorius*
  woodcock, *Scolopax minor*
*Amur honeysuckle, *Lonicera maacki*
Anemone
  rue-, *Anemonella thalictroides*

Common and Scientific Names

Anemone (cont.)
  wood, *Anemone quinquefolia*
Arbor vitae. *See* Cedar, northern white
Arctic
  poppy, *Papaver radicatum*
  primrose, *Primula mistassinica*
  tern, *Sterna paradisaea*
Ash, *Fraxinus* spp.
Ash-leaved maple. *See* Box elder
Aster
  New England, *Aster novae-angliae*
  swamp, *Aster puniceus*
  white, *Aster ericoides*
* Autumn olive, *Elaeagnus umbellata*

B
Bald eagle, *Haliaeetus leucocephalus*
Baltimore oriole, *Icterus galbula*
Baneberry
  red, *Actaea rubra*
  white, *Actaea pachypoda*
Basswood, *Tilia americana*
Bayberry, *Myrica* spp.
Beach sandwort, *Arenaria peploides* var. *diffusa*
Bearberry, *Arctostaphylos uva-ursi*
Beard-tongue, *Penstemon* spp.
Beech, *Fagus grandifolia*
Bellwort, *Uvularia perfoliata*

Belted kingfisher, *Ceryle alcyon*
Bilberry, *Vaccinium uliginosum*
Birch
  bog. *See* swamp
  gray, *Betula populifolia*
  paper. *See* white
  swamp, *Betula pumila*
  white, *Betula papyrifera*
  yellow, *Betula alleghaniensis*
Bird's-eye primrose. *See* Arctic primrose
Black
  cherry, *Prunus serotina*
  crowberry, *Empetrum nigrum*
  *medick, *Medicago lupalina*
  rail, *Laterallus jamaicensis*
  swallowwort, *Cynanchum nigra*
  walnut, *Juglans nigra*
Blackberry, *Rubus allegheniensis*
Black-capped chickadee, *Poecile atricapillus*
Black-eyed Susan, *Rudbeckia hirta*
Black skimmer, *Rynchops niger*
Bladderwort, *Utricularia intermedia*
Blazing star, *Liatris* spp.
Bloodroot, *Sanguinaria canadensis*
Bluebird
  eastern, *Sialia sialis*
  mountain, *Sialia currucoides*
  western, *Sialia mexicana*

Common and Scientific Names

Blue cohosh, *Caulophyllum thalictroides*
Blue-eyed Mary, *Collinsia verna*
Blue-gray gnatcatcher, *Polioptila caerulea*
Blue jay, *Cyanocitta cristata*
Bluets, *Houstonia caerulea*
Bog-rosemary, *Andromeda glaucophylla*
Boneset, *Eupatorium perfoliatum*
Booby, *Sula* spp.
Box
  elder, *Acer negundo*
  turtle, *Terrapene carolina carolina*
Brown
  creeper, *Certhia americana*
  thrasher, *Toxostoma rufum*
Bugleweed, *Lycopus virginianus*
Bunting
  indigo, *Passerina cyanea*
  lazuli, *Passerina amoena*
  snow, *Plectrophenax nivalis*
Buttercup, *Ranunculus* spp.
Butterfly
  eastern tailed blue, *Everes comyntas*
  monarch, *Danaus plexippus*
  spicebush swallowtail, *Papilio troilus*
  sulphur, Subfamily Coliadinae
  viceroy, *Limenitis archippus*
Buttonbush, *Cephalanthus occidentalis*

C

California condor, *Gymnogyps californianus*

Campion

  bladder, *Silene vulgaris*

  moss, *Silene acaulis*

Cardinal-flower, *Lobelia cardinalis*

Caribou, *Rangifer tarandus*

Carrion-flower, *Smilax herbacea*

Catalpa, *Catalpa bignonioides*

* Catnip, *Nepeta cataria*

Cattail

  broad-leaved. *See* common

  common, *Typha latifolia*

  narrow-leaved, *Typha angustifolia*

Cedar

  eastern red, *Juniperus virginiana*

  northern white, *Thuja occidentalis*

Cedar waxwing, *Bombycilla cedrorum*

Cherry

* cornelian, *Cornus mas*

  sand, *Prunus pumila*

Chestnut, *Castanea dentata*

Chickweed, *Stellaria media*

Chicory, *Cichorium intybus*

Club moss

  ground pine, *Lycopodium obscurum*

  shining, *Lycopodium lucidulum*

Common and Scientific Names

Columbine, *Aquilegia canadensis*
Common
  goldeneye, *Bucephala clangula*
  nighthawk, *Chordeiles minor*
  redpoll, *Carduelis flammea*
  yellowthroat, *Geothlypis trichas*
Coneflower, *Ratibida* spp.
Coreopsis
  lance-leaved, *Coreopsis lanceolata*
  prairie, *Coreopsis palmata*
Cotton-grass, *Eriophorum* spp.
Cowbird
  bronzed, *Molothrus aeneus*
  brown-headed, *Molothrus ater*
  shiny, *Molothrus bonariensis*
  South America. *See* shiny
  West Indies. *See* shiny
Cowslip. *See* Marsh-marigold
Cranberry
  high-bush, *Viburnum opulus*
  mountain, *Vaccinium vitis-idaea*
  small, *Vaccinium oxycoccos*
Cranesbill. *See* Wild geranium

D

* Daffodil, *Narcissus* spp.
* Dandelion, *Taraxacum officinale*
Daisy
  English, *Bellis perennis*
* Shasta, *Chrysanthemum* ^x *superbum*
* Dead nettle, *Lamium* spp.
Dogwood
  alternate-leaved, *Cornus alternifolia*
  flowering, *Cornus florida*
  gray, *Cornus racemosa*
  pagoda. *See* alternate-leaved
  panicled. *See* gray
  pink, *Cornus florida* var. *rubra*
  red osier-, *Cornus stolonifera*
Doll's-eyes. *See* Baneberry, white
Double-crested cormorant, *Phalacrocorax auritus*
Douglas fir, *Pseudotsuga taxifolia*
Dove
  mourning, *Zenaida macroura*
  rock, *Columba livia*
Duck
  whistling-tree, *Dendrocygna* spp.
  wood, *Aix sponsa*
Duckweed, *Lemna* spp.
Dutchman's breeches, *Dicentra cucullaria*
Dwarf ginseng, *Panax trifolius*

Common and Scientific Names

E

Eastern
  chipmunk, *Tamias striatus*
  cottontail, *Sylvilagus floridanus*
  cottonwood, *Populus deltoides*
  gray tree frog, *Hyla versicolor*
  hemlock, *Tsuga canadensis*
  meadowlark, *Sturnella magna*
  phoebe, *Sayornis phoebe*
  towhee, *Pipilo erythrophthalmus*
European
* larch, *Larix decidua*
* mountain ash, *Sorbus acuparia*
* starling, *Sturnus vulgaris*

F

Fern
  chain, *Woodwardia virginica*
  Christmas, *Polystichum acrostichoides*
  cinnamon, *Osmunda cinnamomea*
  lady, *Athyrium Filix-femina*
  maidenhair, *Adiantum pedatum*
  northern holly, *Polystichum Braunii*
  sensitive, *Onoclea sensibilis*
  wood, *Dryopteris thelypteris*
Fever bush. *See* Holly, Michigan
Finch
  house, *Carpodacus mexicanus*

Finch (cont.)
  purple, *Carpodacus purpureus*
Fleabane, *Erigeron* spp.
Flycatcher
  Acadian, *Empidonax virescens*
  great crested, *Myiarchus crinitus*
  willow, *Empidonax traillii*
Forget-me-not, *Myosotis* spp.
Fox
  arctic, *Alopex lagopus*
  red, *Vulpes fulva*
Frigatebird, *Fregata* spp.

G

Gambel's quail, *Callipepla gambelii*
*Garlic mustard, *Alliaria petiolata*
Gentian
  closed, *Gentiana andrewsii*
  fringed, *Gentiana crinita*
  horse, *Triosteum perfoliatum*
  lesser fringed, *Gentiana procera*
  soapwort, *Gentiana saponaria*
Ginkgo, *Ginkgo biloba*
*Glossy buckthorn, *Rhamnus frangula*
Golden ragwort, *Senecio aureus*
Goldenrod
  blue-stemmed, *Solidago caesia*
  bog, *Solidago uliginosa*

Common and Scientific Names

Goldenrod (cont.)
  Ohio, *Solidago ohiensis*
  rough-leaved, *Solidago patula*
Grackle, *Quiscalus* spp.
Grape, *Vitis* spp.
Grass
  beach-, *Ammophila breviligulata*
  big bluestem, *Andropogon gerardii*
  blue-eyed-, *Sisyrinchium* spp.
  bottlebrush, *Hystrix patula*
  eel, *Zostera marina*
  Indian, *Sorghastrum nutans*
  marram. *See* beach-
  sour, *Oxalis corniculata*
Grass of Parnassus, *Parnassia glauca*
Gray catbird, *Dumetella carolinensis*
Great water dock, *Rumex orbiculatus*
Greater roadrunner, *Geococcyx californianus*
Grosbeak
  black-headed, *Pheucticus melanocephalus*
  blue, *Guiraca caerulea*
  evening, *Coccothraustes vespertinus*
  rose-breasted, *Pheucticus ludovicianus*
Gum
  black, *Nyssa sylvatica*
  sour. *See* black
  sweet, *Liquidambar styraciflua*
Gyrfalcon, *Falco rusticolus*

H

Harbinger of spring, *Erigenia bulbosa*
Hardhack, *Spirea tomentosa*
Harebell, *Campanula rotundifolia*
Hawk
  Cooper's, *Accipiter cooperii*
  red-tailed, *Buteo jamaicensis*
  rough-legged, *Buteo lagopus*
  sharp-shinned, *Accipiter striatus*
  sparrow. *See* American kestrel
Hawthorn, *Crataegus* spp.
*Heal-all, *Prunella vulgaris*
Heath family, Ericaceae
Hepatica
  round-lobed, *Hepatica americana*
  sharp-lobed, *Hepatica acutiloba*
Heron
  great blue, *Ardea herodias*
  little blue, *Egretta caerulea*
Hickory
  pignut, *Carya glabra*
  shagbark, *Carya ovata*
High-bush blueberry, *Vaccinium corymbosum*
Holly
  American, *Ilex opaca*
  Michigan, *Ilex verticillata*
  mountain, *Nemopanthus mucronatus*
  southern, *Ilex vomitaria*

Common and Scientific Names

Hop hornbeam, *Ostrya virginiana*
Horned lark, *Eremophila alpestris*
* Horse-chestnut, *Aesculus hippocastanum*
Horsetail, *Equisetum* spp.
Hummingbird
  blue-throated, *Lampornis clemenciae*
  ruby-throated, *Archilochus colubris*

I

Impatiens. See Jewel-weed
Indian pipe, *Monotropa uniflora*
Inkberry. *See* Pokeweed
Inky cap mushroom, *Coprinus atramentarius*
Innocence. *See* Bluets
Ironweed, *Vernonia fasciculata*
Isabella moth, Subfamily Arctiinae
Ivory gull, *Pagophila eburnea*

J

Jack-in-the-pulpit, *Arisaema triphyllum*
* Japanese barberry, *Berberis thunbergii*
Joe Pye weed, *Eupatorium maculatum*
Junco
  dark-eyed, *Junco hyemalis*
  slate-colored. *See* dark-eyed
Juniper, *Juniperus* spp.

K

Kentucky coffee tree, *Gymnocladus dioica*
Killdeer, *Charadrius vociferus*
Kinglet
  golden-crowned, *Regulus satrapa*
  ruby-crowned, *Regulus calendula*

L

Labrador tea, *Ledum groenlandicum*
Lady-slipper. *See under* Orchid
Lapland
  longspur, *Calcarius lapponicus*
  lousewort, *Pedicularis lanata*
Leatherleaf, *Chamaedaphne calyculata*
Lily
* blackberry, *Belamcanda chinensis*
  fawn. *See* trout
  trout, *Erythronium americanum*
Lingonberry, *Vaccinium vitis-idaea* var. *minus*
Lobelia
  brook, *Lobelia kalmii*
  great blue, *Lobelia siphilitica*
  Kalm's. *See* brook
Locust
  black, *Robinia pseudoacacia*
  honey, *Gleditsia triacanthos*
Log-cock. *See* Woodpecker, pileated
Longtail weasel, *Mustela frenata*

Common and Scientific Names

Loon
  common, *Gavia immer*
  red-throated, *Gavia stellata*

M

Maidenhair. *See* Ginkgo
Mallard, *Anas platyrhyncos*
Maple
* Japanese, *Acer palmatum*
* Norway, *Acer platanoides*
  red, *Acer rubrum*
  sugar, *Acer saccharinum*
Maple-leaved viburnum, *Viburnum acerifolium*
Marsh-marigold, *Caltha palustris*
May apple, *Podophyllum peltatum*
Merganser
  common, *Mergus merganser*
  hooded, *Lophodytes cucullatus*
  red-breasted, *Mergus serrator*
Mint
  horse, *Monarda punctata*
  mountain, *Pycnanthemum* spp.
Moccasin-flower. *See under* Orchid, lady slipper, pink
Morning glory, *Ipomoea tricolor*
Mountain avens, *Dryas integrifolia*
Mourning cloak, *Nymphalis antiopa*
Mulberry, *Morus* spp.
Mute swan, *Cygnus olor*

N

Nightshade
  black, *Solanum dulcamara*
  common. *See* black
Nodding ladies-tresses. *See under* Orchid
Northern
  cardinal, *Cardinalis cardinalis*
  flicker, *Colaptes auratus*
  gannet, *Morus bassanus*
  hackberry, *Celtis occidentalis*
  mockingbird, *Mimus polyglottos*
  oriole. *See* Baltimore oriole
  spring peeper, *Pseudacris crucifer crucifer*
  waterthrush, *Seirurus noveboracensis*
  wheatear, *Oenanthe oenanthe*
Nuthatch
  red-breasted, *Sitta canadensis*
  white-breasted, *Sitta carolinensis*

O

Oak
  black, *Quercus velutina*
  bur, *Quercus macrocarpa*
  chinquapin, *Quercus muehlenbergii*
  pin, *Quercus palustris*
  red, *Quercus rubra*
  shingle, *Quercus imbricaria*
  white, *Quercus alba*

Common and Scientific Names

Old man's beard. *See* Virgin's bower
Opossum, *Didelphis marsupialis*
Orchid
  lady-slipper
    pink, *Cypripedium acaule*
    showy, *Cypripedium reginae*
    white, *Cypripedium candidum*
    yellow, *Cypripedium calceolus*
  moccasin-flower. *See* lady-slipper, pink
  nodding ladies-tresses, *Spiranthes cernua*
  orange-fringed, *Platanthera ciliaris*
  yellow-fringed, *Habenaria ciliaris*
Osage orange tree, *Maclura pomifera*
Owl
  barn, *Tyto alba*
  barred, *Strix varia*
  eastern screech, *Otus asio*
  great gray, *Strix nebulosa*
  great horned, *Bubo virginianus*
  long-eared, *Asio otus*
  snowy, *Nyctea scandiaca*

P

Partridge-berry, *Mitchella repens*
Passenger pigeon, *Ectopistes migratorius*
Pawpaw, *Asimina triloba*
Pear, *Pyrus communis*
Pepper and salt. *See* Harbinger of spring

* Peppermint, *Mentha* ^{x} *piperita*
* Perennial pea, *Lathyrus latifolius*
Phalarope, *Phalaropus* spp.
Pickerel-weed, *Pontederia cordata*
Pied-billed grebe, *Podilymbus podiceps*
Pigeon berry. *See* Pokeweed
Pine

  bristlecone, *Pinus aristata*
  eastern white, *Pinus strobus*
  jack, *Pinus banksiana*
  Jeffrey, *Pinus jeffreyi*
  ponderosa. *See* western yellow
  western yellow, *Pinus ponderosa*
Pine siskin, *Carduelis pinus*
Pink

  gerardia, *Agalinis* spp.
  lady-slipper. *See under* Orchid
Pitcher-plant, *Sarracenia purpurea*
Pleurisy root. *See* Weed, butterfly
Pokeberry. *See* Pokeweed
Pokeweed, *Phytolacca americana*
Polar bear, *Ursus maritimus*
Prairie

  crab, *Malus ioënsis*
  smoke, *Anemone patens*
* Purple loosestrife, *Lythrum salicaria*

Common and Scientific Names

Q
Quaker lady. *See* Bluets
* Queen Anne's lace, *Daucus carota*

R
Rabbit. *See* Eastern cottontail
Raccoon, *Procyon lotor*
Ragweed, *Ambrosia artemisiifolia*
Raven
  Chihuahuan, *Corvus cryptoleucus*
  common, *Corvus corax*
  white-necked. *See* Chihuahuan
Red-berried elder, *Sambucus racemosa*
Redbud, *Cercis canadensis*
Red-winged blackbird, *Agelaius phoeniceus*
* Ring-necked pheasant, *Phasianus colchicus*
Rocket
  sea, *Cakile edentula*
  yellow, *Barbarea vulgaris*
Rose
* multiflora, *Rosa multiflora*
  swamp, *Rosa palustris*
Rosemary, *Andromeda polifolia*
Rose-pink, *Sabatia angularis*
Ruffed grouse, *Bonasa umbellus*
Rufous-sided towhee. *See* Eastern towhee

Rush
  baltic, *Juncus balticus*
  chairmaker's, *Scirpus americanus*
  spike, *Eleocharis* spp.

S

Saguaro, *Carnegiea gigantean*
St. John's wort
  marsh, *Hypericum virginicum*
  spotted, *Hypericum punctatum*
Sandhill crane, *Grus canadensis*
Sassafras, *Sassafras albidum*
Saxifrage
  prickly, *Saxifraga tricuspidata*
  purple, *Saxifraga oppositifolia*
Scarlet
  cup, *Sarcoscypha coccinea*
  tanager, *Piranga olivacea*
Sea lungwort, *Mertensia maritima*
Serviceberry, *Amelanchier* spp.
Shadbush. *See* Serviceberry
Shrubby cinquefoil, *Potentilla fruticosa*
Skunk cabbage, *Symplocarpus foetidus*
Skylark, *Alauda arvensis*
Smooth spiderwort, *Tradescantia ohiensis*
*Snowdrop, *Galanthus nivalis*
Snow flea, *Collembola* spp.
Snowshoe hare, *Lepus americanus*

Common and Scientific Names

Solomon's seal, *Polygonatum pubescens*
  plumy false, *Smilacina racemosa*
  starry false, *Smilacina stellata*
Sparrow
  American tree, *Spizella arborea*
  field, *Spizella pusilla*
  grasshopper, *Ammodramus savannarum*
  house, *Passer domesticus*
  song, *Melospiza melodia*
  white-throated, *Zonotrichia albicollis*
Spatterdock, *Nuphar advena*
Spicebush, *Lindera benzoin*
Spike-moss, *Selaginella* spp.
Spotted
  jewel-weed, *Impatiens capensis*
* knapweed, *Centaurea maculosa*
Spreading dogbane, *Apocynum androsaemifolium*
Spring-beauty, *Claytonia virginica*
Spruce, *Picea* spp.
Squirrel
  black. *See* eastern gray
  eastern fox, *Sciurus niger*
  eastern gray, *Sciurus carolinensis*
  red, *Tamiasciurus hudsonicus*
  southern flying, *Glaucomys volans*
  thirteen-lined ground, *Citellus tridecemlineatus*
Squirrel corn, *Dicentia canadensis*
Steeplebush. *See* Hardhack

Strawberry, *Fragaria virginiana*
Sumac
  dwarf. *See* shining
  fragrant, *Rhus aromatica*
  poison, *Toxicodendron vernix*
  shining, *Rhus copallina*
  smooth, *Rhus glabra*
  staghorn, *Rhus typhina*
  velvet. *See* staghorn
Sundew, *Drosera* spp.
Swallow
  barn, *Hirundo rustica*
  tree, *Tachycineta bicolor*
Swamp
  dock, *Diapensia lapponica*
  milkweed, *Asclepias incarnata*
  thistle, *Cirsium muticum*
Sweet
  Cicely, *Osmorhiza* spp.
*William, *Dianthus barbatus*
Sycamore, *Platanus occidentalis*

T
Tamarack, *Larix laricina*
Thimbleweed, *Anemone virginiana*
Thrift, *Armeria maritima*

Common and Scientific Names

Thrush
  gray-cheeked, *Catharus minimus*
  hermit, *Catharus guttatus*
  wood, *Catharus mustelina*
Titmouse
  bridled, *Baeolophus wollweberi*
  oak, *Baeolophus inornatus*
  plain. *See* oak
  tufted, *Baeolophus bicolor*
Toad, *Bufo* spp.
Toothwort
  cut-leaved, *Dentaria laciniata*
  two-leaved*, Dentaria diphylla*
Touch-me-not. *See* Jewel-weed, spotted
Trailing arbutus, *Epigaea repens*
Trillium
  big white, *Trillium grandiflorum*
  nodding, *Trillium cernuum*
  red, *Trillium erectum*
  yellow, *Trillium sessile*
Tulip tree, *Liriodendron tulipifera*
Twinflower, *Linnaea borealis*

V

Veery, *Catharus fuscescens*
Violet
  birdfoot, *Viola pedata*
  common blue, *Viola pensylvanica*

Violet (cont.)
  dog tooth. *See* Lily, trout
  lance-leaved, *Viola lanceolata*
  long-spurred, *Viola rostrata*
  northern white, *Viola pallens*
  yellow, *Viola pubescens*
Vireo
  bell's, *Vireo bellii*
  black-capped, *Vireo atricapillus*
  gray, *Vireo vicinior*
  Philadelphia, *Vireo philadelphicus*
  red-eyed, *Vireo olivaceus*
  warbling, *Vireo gilvus*
  yellow-throated, *Vireo flavifrons*
Virginia bluebell, *Mertensia virginica*
Virginia waterleaf, *Hydrophyllum virginianum*
Virgin's bower, *Clematis virginiana*

W

Warbler
  black-and-white, *Mniotilta varia*
  blackburnian, *Dendroica fusco*
  black-throated blue, *Dendroica caerulescens*
  blue-winged, *Vermivora pinus*
  golden-cheeked, *Dendroica chrysoparia*
  golden-winged, *Vermivora chrysoptera*
  hooded, *Wilsonia citrina*
  Kirtland's, *Dendroica kirtlandii*

Common and Scientific Names

Warbler (cont.)
 magnolia, *Dendroica magnolia*
 Nashville, *Vermivora ruficapilla*
 pine, *Dendroica pinus*
 Tennessee, *Vermivora peregrina*
 worm-eating, *Helmitheros vermivorus*
 yellow, *Dendroica petechia*
 yellow-rumped, *Dendroica coronata*
 yellow-throated, *Dendroica dominica*
*Watercress, *Rorippa nasturtium-aquaticum*
Water horehound, *Lycopus* spp.
Weed
 butterfly, *Asclepias tuberosa*
 tinker's. *See* Gentian, horse
White-footed mouse, *Peromyscus leucopus*
White heather, *Cassiope tetragona*
White-winged crossbill, *Loxia leucoptera*
Widow's tear. *See* Spiderwort, smooth
Wild
 bergamot, *Monarda fistulosa*
 blue phlox, *Phlox divaricata*
 clematis. *See* Virgin's bower
 geranium, *Geranium maculatum*
 ginger, *Asarum canadense*
 leek, *Allium tricocccum*
 turkey, *Meleagris gallopavo*

Willow
  black, *Salix nigra*
  blueleaf, *Salix myricoides*
  hoary, *Salix candida*
  prairie, *Salix humilis*
  pussy-, *Salix discolor*
  water, *Decodon verticillatus*
*weeping, *Salix babylonica*
Willow ptarmigan, *Lagopus lagopus*
Winterberry. *See* Holly, Michigan
*Wintercress, *Barbarea vulgaris*
Witch-hazel, *Hamamelis virginiana*
  vernal, *Hamamelis vernalis*
Wood betony, *Pedicularis canadensis*
Woodchuck, *Marmota monax*
Woodpecker
  acorn, *Melanerpes formicivorus*
  black-backed, *Picoides arcticus*
  downy, *Picoides pubescens*
  hairy, *Picoides villosus*
  ivory-billed, *Campephilus principalis*
  pileated, *Dryocopus pileatus*
  red-bellied, *Melanerpes carolinus*
  red-headed, *Melanerpes erythrocephalus*
Wood stork, *Mycteria americana*
Wooly bear caterpillar, Subfamily Arctiinae
Wormwood, *Artemisia* spp.

Common and Scientific Names

Wren
  Carolina, *Thryothorus ludovicianus*
  house, *Troglodytes aedon*
  winter, *Troglodytes troglodytes*

Y

Yellow-bellied sapsucker, *Sphyrapicus varius*
*Yellow rocket. *See* Wintercress
Yew, *Taxus canadensis*

Index

*The names of many trees are not indexed separately
but are found under the main heading,* Tree.

Index

Index

Dogwood, 48, 89-93
  alternate-leaved, 91
  flowering, 204
  fruit, 89, 117-18
  gray, 91
  pagoda. *See* alternate-
    leaved
  panicled. *See* gray
  pink, 188
  red osier-, 84, 85, 91
Doll's-eyes.
  See Baneberry, white
Duck
  whistling-tree, 99
  wood, 98
Dumas, Alexander, 231
Dutchman's breeches, 147,
  166

E

Eastman, John, 274
  describes: black locust
  seeds 125, cattail seeds
  270, corn grains storage
  271, dogwood fruit 89,
  eastern white pine 106,
  108, flowering dogwood
  fruits 117, hazelnut catkin 124, ruby-throated
  hummingbird food 27,
  spotted jewel-weed seeds
  184-85, titmouse longevity record 61, titmouse
  nest 60, use of hepatica
  root tea 151, winterberry
    associates 136
Emerson, Ralph Waldo,
  176
Evers, Dave, 45

F

Fawn lily. *See* Lily, trout
Felsing, John, 26
Fen, 197-201
Fern
  Christmas, 261
  sensitive, 261
  wood, 261
Fever bush. *See* Holly,
  Michigan
Flea, snow, 263
Flower colors, examples of
  black, 230-31
  blue, 174-76
  orange, 182-84
  pale pink, 186-88, 189

Index

Index

Index

Index